WHAT ARE WE CHASING?

WHAT ARE WE CHASING?

JOE COLETTI

 New Harbor Press

What Are We Chasing?
Copyright © 2017 by Joe Coletti.

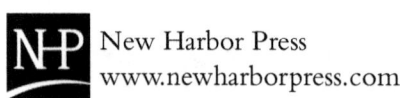 New Harbor Press
www.newharborpress.com

All rights reserved. Printed in the United States of America. No part of this book may be used or reproduced in any manner whatsoever without written permission except in the case of brief quotations embodied in critical articles or reviews.

This book is a work of fiction. Names, characters, businesses, organizations, places, events and incidents either are the product of the author's imagination or are used fictitiously. Any resemblance to actual persons, living or dead, events, or locales is entirely coincidental.

Printed in the United States of America. All rights reserved under International Copyright Law.

ISBN 978-1-63357-109-9

Library of Congress Control Number: 2017936937

CONTENTS

INTRODUCTION 1

1) THE MIRROR 3

2) RELATIONSHIPS 21

3) PARENTING 35

4) MONEY 49

5) FAITH 63

6) MARRIAGE 81

7) ACCEPTANCE 91

8) HUMILITY 105

9) THE CHANGE 113

INTRODUCTION

IN OUR CURRENT CULTURE made up of the most advanced technology, social communication, ability to self-promote, and any other noise that competes for our time and energy, it is becoming increasingly more difficult to decipher the real truths in our own lives. The inspiration of this book comes from the realization of what gets lost in the shuffle of our own lives while we are busy trying to do and have a million things all at the same time.

As we are so busy trying to accumulate everything we can and working our way up the perceived cultural ladder, what are we missing along the way? The odds are that I have surpassed the midpoint of my existence here in this life, and the closer I get to not being here anymore, the clearer life becomes to me. It's too bad it takes us so long. I am sure there are a select few who realize what's important early in life, but I would say for most of us, not so much. We deceive and convince ourselves that we haven't bought into the ways of our secular culture. Our mortality is real, and my hope is that our culture will see that again one day. We should live our lives to the fullest, make the most of our opportunities, and strive to be successful, but

WHAT ARE WE CHASING?

at what expense? Should it be at the expense of others, or even our own peace and true happiness?

The ways of the culture had me fooled for a long time: be successful, have a big house, have the best cars, the best clothes, and teach my kids all the same things. Teach my kids that if they don't do everything to keep up with everybody, they will be left in the dust. Really? The truth is no matter how much we achieve or attain, we will all be left in the dust eventually. We only have eighty to ninety years if we're lucky.

No matter how long we are here on this earth, every day is one day closer to not being here. Our time will come eventually, and we can leave behind a bunch of material possessions and broken relationships, or we can leave behind a legacy. Leaving behind a legacy doesn't have to be a big thing either. It could be just leaving with our family and friends knowing that maybe we weren't perfect, but we loved them and we hope they can live a life trying to do the same for others. For me, this book is a reality check into how the culture persuades us to see things as opposed to seeing how they really are. The culture places such emphasis on things that, eventually, we will come to learn have very little importance whatsoever. We do things based on what everyone else thinks we should do or how we want people to see us, instead of doing what our heart tells us to do. At some point, I think we have to take a good hard look at ourselves, forget about all that stuff our culture teaches us, and then the next morning do it all over again, because the culture will come right back at us. It is hard to see ourselves as we really are, but I would recommend that you try. My hope is that this book helps to open our hearts, minds, and souls to the truth, whatever that may be in each of our own lives.

1

The Mirror

AS A FORTY-FIVE-YEAR-OLD FATHER of four, I have certainly had my share of different experiences in my lifetime. I was in the business world for many years, I have been a stay-at-home dad for many years. I was single until I was twenty-nine; now, I have been married for sixteen years. My first child, once a baby, is just weeks away from getting her driver's permit. It's funny when you look back how much you can see. If only it could be that clear when we are in the middle of it.

I know when I look in the mirror today I do not see what I used to see. It's funny, because one thing most of us do every day is look in the mirror. At some point, when getting ready for work, getting ready for school, getting ready to go out, we will look in the mirror each day. The question is: what do we

WHAT ARE WE CHASING?

see? Is what you see today the same thing as what you saw yesterday?

Our actions from the previous day can certainly change the way we see ourselves the next day in the mirror. Sure, we may look the same, but our actions determine how we see ourselves. Of course, that can be really good, or really bad. We get an opportunity each time we look in the mirror to see ourselves, to be completely honest with ourselves. Or we can convince ourselves that everything we are doing is great, and we can go on being who we are. The truth is if we are being honest, I am sure we could each find a thing or two about ourselves that could use a little work…or a lot of work. For some reason, though, we find it hard to be honest with ourselves. We have this ability to deceive ourselves and convince ourselves that everything is fine, and that some of the situations we have gotten ourselves involved in are "not that bad."

It is interesting to think of the reasons that make it so hard to be honest with ourselves. I am not saying that we are never honest with ourselves, but that honesty usually comes after long periods of time when we are not, and that has put us in a position where we have to be. For example, if a person has an addictive habit, whatever it is—drugs, alcohol, gambling, etc.—it usually takes hitting rock bottom to see the situation as it really is. One day, that habit has caused them to miss their rent enough to be evicted, or that habit has alienated away family members whom they may have been closest to. This habit may have gone on for twenty years with the person convincing themselves, totally deceiving themselves, that everything was all right. When they finally get evicted, lose a job or alienate family enough to where they felt like they need to keep their distance from that person, they may finally have the opportunity to be honest with themselves. That person may then look back at the past twenty years and realize what he has cost himself by not being honest with himself a lot sooner.

This has nothing to do with being dishonest with others; it is about being dishonest with yourself. What makes it so hard to be honest with ourselves? I think that in our current culture, we tend to walk around being extremely concerned about what other people think of us. We probably would not even be honest with ourselves about that. How many times have you heard someone say, or better yet, how many times have you said, "I don't care what anyone else thinks"? Many people go around saying that, but the majority of us, if we are being honest with ourselves, do not live that way. So if we are walking around worrying about what others think, how others see us, or if we have what others have, we tend to reach for things that really are not even that important to us. But we reach for them anyway, just because we want to appear a certain way to others. Why do we do that?

It's funny I have a twelve-year-old daughter, my second child, and without being biased, I tell you she is a beautiful, talented, thoughtful, and caring person. She is glad to help anybody with anything, and can't stand to see anyone suffer, even if it is just a paper cut on their finger. But she always seems to be concerned about what others think of her or who may or may not like her. As a parent, one of the biggest points my wife and I try to get across to her is that it doesn't matter what anyone else thinks. I think most parents would agree they would try to convey this to their child as well. As parents we see our children as unique, smart, and beautiful all in their own way, just the way they are, but sometimes we can't even look at ourselves as being all those things just the way we are.

The reason we try to appear a certain way to others is because we know better than anyone else what our faults and failures are. On those few occasions we do look in the mirror honestly, we see what our faults and failures are. For some reason, unlike the child we try to convince is perfect just the way they are, we try to walk around as if everything is perfect all the time, and we want to appear as if we always have it all together. This is quite contradictory to when we say, "I don't care what anyone else thinks." The truth is we do care; we are human, and the sooner we admit that, the sooner we can do something about it.

Recall the addict who has hit rock bottom, and now has to be honest with himself. If the addict never admitted that they have a problem, they will never be able to do anything about it. Of course, who wants to be seen as someone that has a problem? That is one of the big reasons that they will not admit the problem. We go around acting as everything is fine all the time because we don't want people to see our faults and failures.

Most of the time when we look in the mirror, we don't even want to see those faults and failures ourselves. How is it that everyone walks around as if everything is fine all the time, yet one of two marriages end in divorce, there is a high rate of teen suicide, domestic violence is off the charts, obesity, depression—we can go on and on. Looking at yourself in the mirror honestly takes courage. Maybe not just looking in the mirror, but looking in the mirror while being honest and doing something about it. Working on your faults and failures in the midst of not worrying about what anyone else thinks is a powerful transformation you can make for yourself.

There are people in our lives whom we have known for years yet do not know us for who we truly are. They only know who we have led them to believe we are. The reason it takes so much courage is because making these changes for ourselves may affect relationships we have with others in many ways. Others will notice some differences in you and may or may not like them. We may lose a friend we thought was a good friend because they may not be comfortable with the changes they see in us. How good of a friend was that? If you come to the point where you are completely honest with yourself all the time and are trying to better yourself and be more conscious of each decision you make, and somebody is not comfortable with that, maybe that is not who you should be surrounding yourself with. A true friend will accept the fact that you are trying to grow and improve yourself. Unfortunately, it doesn't always work like that, but we have to have the courage to be all right with that.

On the other hand, a change in ourselves may inspire a positive change in someone else in your life. Generally speaking, when we are honest with ourselves and try to better ourselves, we tend to do much more positive things. We tend to be more helpful, we become better listeners, we become better parents, better friends, and we are more conscious of our thoughts, words, and actions more so than if we were not being honest with ourselves. One thing being honest with ourselves helps us do is be more accountable to ourselves. I think we can agree that accountability is not at the top of the list in our current culture. It is a rare occasion when somebody takes responsibility for anything that has gone wrong. Our culture is not quick to admit its mistakes, but you can certainly find plenty of people telling you whose fault it was.

It goes back to the same premise. We have such a hard time being honest with ourselves, so much so that it is difficult to admit our mistakes. We don't like to make mistakes but, as humans, we may as well accept the fact that they are going to happen. Some of them will be huge. The truth is that the sooner we are honest with ourselves and can admit our mistakes, the quicker we can recover from them. Some mistakes cause pain to others and some mistakes cause pain to ourselves. We know instantly when we have hurt others or ourselves, but we hang on to it and hope it goes away. Good luck with that. Try looking in the mirror every day, hanging on to one of those huge hurtful mistakes all to yourself. It will eat away at you like termites on one of those hundred-year-old houses on a home improvement show.

Another reason it takes courage to be honest with yourself is because it will force you to be honest with others. You will be forced to be more honest with your spouse, your friends, your children, your coworkers, and anybody that you have any kind of relationship with. Sometimes it is extremely hard to be honest with the people you are closest to. You don't want to hurt them, and you may be concerned that being honest with them will affect how they feel about you. It is a legitimate fear and, again, part of the reason we struggle to be honest with ourselves. I think most would agree that being truly honest with others in relationships, in the long run, would certainly be for the best and enhance the relationship. The mirror is a great opportunity every day to assess our own progress against our weaknesses. We could look in the mirror at seven o' clock in the morning and go about our business for the day, and then come back and look in the mirror at seven o' clock in the evening to determine whether or not we have changed for the better or worse in those last twelve hours. We can reflect on what opportunities we had to be honest with ourselves and others during that same period of time.

Imagine holding ourselves accountable every time we looked in the mirror, intentionally making an effort to discern what we have or have not done since the last time we looked in the mirror. If we constantly assess our own accountability for our actions—without any biases or influences, with complete honesty—our natural instinct will be to make better choices, because we have to answer to ourselves for the actions we take. One of the things needed to make this successful for ourselves is to understand that if we honestly look and assess our actions on a regular basis, we are forced to accept the fact that sometimes we will still make bad choices, and we will have to answer to ourselves for those choices. The thing about holding ourselves accountable is that we make a conscious effort to make better decisions on a daily basis. It is much easier to look at ourselves when we have spent our time making better decisions that lead to truthful happiness, as opposed to making questionable decisions based on instant gratification or pleasure.

WHAT ARE WE CHASING?

For instance, imagine during that twelve-hour period you are going through a regular day at work and you have a meeting. Your office has supplied some refreshments for the meeting. On one tray of refreshments are donuts and cookies, and on another tray are some bananas and apples. To drink, you have to choose between Coke and water. Now, I don't know about you, but for me and probably most of us, the donuts and Coke look much more appealing than fruit and water. Most of the time, our first thought would be to choose a donut or two because it would provide instant gratification. If we are being honest, it will taste way better than one of those bananas or apples. Now when we look at ourselves in the mirror that evening, will we feel good about that decision? On the other hand, if we chose a piece of fruit and a water, wouldn't we know that we made a better decision? Sure, this is a small decision, one of many small decisions we make each day, but they all have an effect on us.

Let's say on the way home from work that day you pass an elderly person broken down on the side of the road, in need of obvious assistance. Most of the time we are so focused on where we are going and what we are doing that we will drive right by. Most of us will consider stopping to help, but usually we will just keep on going. We make that decision to keep going. Now imagine if we decided to stop and take thirty minutes out of our day to help this person—how good does that decision make you feel? How will you feel looking in the mirror assessing that decision? Also think of the effect it will have on others when you get home. You could tell your children that you got home later that evening because you stopped to help somebody. Now you have an opportunity to teach your kids the importance of helping someone. You will actually feel better for taking the time away from your self-absorbed where-am-I-going and what-do-I-have-to-do-for-myself thoughts to help someone else. I am not saying that it is realistic to think that we could always be the one who can stop and help that person—we may have an appointment, a family event, or a child's ballgame to get to—but when the opportunity arises when we can help, do we? I am not saying that it is always wrong if we choose that donut and a Coke for a snack over the fruit and water, but if we do that every day, with lack of self-control or accountability, then it becomes something to think about. Everything is relevant. If we are generally healthy, eat well, and make an effort to exercise here and there, that donut and Coke as an occasional choice is fine.

The thing is we know ourselves well enough to know when we look in the mirror what good and bad decisions we have made that day. The key is to be honest with ourselves about it. There is no other human being who really matters other than yourself who can hold you accountable for your actions. Sure we have bosses, teachers, and other people of authority in our lives that will hold us accountable, but it really does not make a difference if you are holding yourself accountable. At that point, it doesn't matter what anyone else thinks. In fact, if your boss or your teacher sees how you hold yourself accountable and that you take responsibility for your own actions, they are less likely to be looking over your shoulder or concerned about the work you are doing, which in turn makes their job easier and more productive.

WHAT ARE WE CHASING?

Most of our decisions clearly affect more than just us, but that is usually the farthest thing from our mind. Think about that person on the side of the road that you stopped to help. Not only does that help the person, but something about having someone go out of their way and help you like that makes the person being helped feel a sense of gratitude, which is one of the best ways to feel. Being grateful sparks so many other positive feelings and emotions. Let's say the first thing you do when you wake up in the morning is reflect on the things you are grateful for. You can't help but start your day in a positive manner. No matter what struggles we have going on in our lives, we all have things to be grateful for. By intentionally waking up and starting each day by reflecting on what we are grateful for, we start our day with thoughts that fill our hearts with things that put us in a positive mindset. A mother who stays home with her children may feel less anxiety or stress looking at a mess her children have left before heading to school, even after they were told to clean it up, because she just finished reflecting on how thankful she is to have these children. That does not mean she will not address the situation when they come home, but it is a lot less of a burden to address the situation in a calm, nonstressful manner when in some circumstances this may want to make her pull her hair out. Meanwhile her husband is up getting ready for work after he has reflected on what he is thankful for. As he sits at the table drinking his coffee, one of these children he has just reflected on being grateful for spills milk all over the suit he was wearing to work that day, because the child was horsing around with his brother. How many reactions can there be to this situation? Dad may want to grab these kids by the shirt collars and bang their heads together, he may go into panic mode because now he is going to be late for the job that he has just reflected on being grateful for, or he may calmly get up, tell his boys that they will be discussing this later, change, and go to work. Being calm and going to work after that fiasco is more likely to happen if you are in a state of mind of appreciation.

That same guy on the side of the road that you stopped to help now gets back in his car and heads home. A car blatantly cuts him off, makes it through a traffic light which is about to turn red, causing him to miss the light. Normally, a circumstance like this can cause a variety of negative reactions, but because he is in the state of mind of appreciation and gratitude, it tends not to bother him. In fact, he may even have the thought that the guy that cut him off may have some reason to be in such a hurry, and he is glad he was able to make it through that light. This is what being grateful does for us.

Take a few minutes each morning before you get started, look in the mirror, reflect on what you are grateful for, and pray about it. State of mind is a powerful contributor to how your day is going to turn out. If you wake up and you're thinking, *I have to go to work, I have all these boring meetings today, and I have to meet that guy who talks too much.* How do you think that day is going to turn out? Now if you go into the day thinking, *I am looking forward to seeing how these meetings can help us improve something, I am going to smile at the guy who talks too much, and really listen to what he has to say and see if I can pick up any information that can help the company.* State of mind is a powerful

WHAT ARE WE CHASING?

thing. Part of the result of your day is determined by your state of mind going into that day.

Wouldn't you rather give yourself a better chance at a successful day? Especially if a couple of simple habit changes is all it takes. Simple habit changes can make great life changes.

Let's say as a habit, you come home from work every day, sit on the couch, grab a beer or two, and turn on the television for an hour before dinner. It just kind of becomes what you are accustomed to doing. Now, let's say you decide to make a habit change one day and you start coming home from work and instead of grabbing that beer and sitting on the couch, you take a walk for ten or fifteen minutes, and then maybe you come back and read a good book for ten or fifteen minutes. These simple habit changes can have an extremely positive effect on you. Instead of mindlessly sitting there on the couch and feeling kind of lazy, you now have gotten a little exercise and stimulated your mind in that same period of time. You did not overexert yourself or do anything crazy, you just made a simple change in your habit. In the long run, it is easy to see which one makes for a better habit. We fail sometimes to realize that it really is that simple. Now imagine changing a few habits like this over a period of time. How much improvement could we each make to our lives with some simple habit changes? I believe *simple* is the key word here. We can all make simple changes. We can all use a little more simplicity in our lives, period. Our culture seems to put so much importance on how busy we are and how many things we have, as if that makes us better people. We live such complex lives that involve something to do every second of every day, which makes it even harder to stop, take a breath, and take a good honest look at ourselves in the mirror. Half of the time we are complaining about how busy we are and all we have to do. Meanwhile, we brought most of it upon ourselves by choice in the first place.

Our culture has taught us that if we are not busy or striving to get, or be, the next greatest thing every second of every day, then we are wasting time and missing opportunities. We run around like crazy, filling our lives with unnecessary busyness just because we think that is what we are supposed to do. We struggle to find time to just take a breath, sit quietly, and regroup. Think about it: as a culture, why don't we eat well? Why don't we exercise more? Why don't we spend more time with friends and family? We are too busy! Too busy doing what? Well, if we have acknowledged our weakness as humans to be worried about what everyone else thinks, we can address some of the problem. We spend so much time trying to look good to others, and I don't mean in an appearance sense.

Our technological world is a great example. People are walking around with six-hundred-dollar smartphones. Why do so many people feel the need to have a six-hundred-dollar phone? Most people do not even use half of the features that make the phone cost that much, but they can say they have one. The worst part is that in a year, a new one will come out and everyone will be chasing that. The same goes for computers, televisions, and any other technology that will constantly be trying to convince us that the next thing coming out is the best thing ever… until next year anyway. Our culture leads us to believe that we always need to have the best of whatever it is coming out or we will be fools. When we get these new

WHAT ARE WE CHASING?

gadgets, we show them to people and talk about how great they are and how much they can do. We are so proud; it's as if we are talking about a new child. When we look in the mirror, will we see that we are happier because we have this new phone or whatever it may be? No, but you actually feel relieved that you don't have to be the embarrassed person who doesn't have one. There we go again, worrying about what everyone else thinks. Human nature is so peculiar.

We struggle to not worry about what everyone else thinks—everyone else who, for the most part, have no relevance in our life and never will. What does it take to not worry about what anyone else thinks? Can you think back to when you were a child? Most of us have specific memories that, for one reason or another, stand out, and a lot of them were from a time of carefree behavior that we realize we could never duplicate as an adult. I wonder what age we have to get to before we start being concerned with what anyone else thinks. I look at my eight-year-old son as an example. He is a typical eight-year-old boy who loves to be outside, run around, get dirty, play baseball, etc. Now, if he were to walk through a mud puddle with his good pants on and it messed them up pretty good, that would really have no effect on him. He would go to school, church, wherever, just looking like that if we let him. What anyone else around him thinks he could care less. Now if that happened to my fourteen-year-old daughter, she would have to get that straight before she crossed the street. *At some point it changes.* You become conscious of what people see you doing, what they see you wearing, how you present yourself in general.

The funny thing is that at some point, we will stop concerning ourselves with that again one day. I'll give you an example.

An elderly gentleman walks into a grocery store to get a few items that his wife no doubt sent him out for. This guy walks into the store wearing khaki shorts that almost reach his knees, white socks that almost reach his shorts, black shoes, a tucked-in plaid button-down short sleeve shirt, and a belt that he buckles on the same buckle he had it set on twenty-five years ago. He is wearing some kind of hat, maybe it says something about fishing or his favorite sports team. This guy looks ridiculous. We have all seen this guy. This guy could care less. Now we may look at him and laugh a little, or tap our spouse or our friend on the shoulder and have a little chuckle with them about it, but he doesn't care about that either. The even better thing about this guy is that he gets a chuckle at our expense. Let me tell you why.

One thing about people who are elderly or older than us is that they have been where we are. We generally don't ever picture ourselves as an elderly person. When we are growing up in school, we can picture ourselves in the lives we are striving to achieve, whether that is a becoming a businessperson, having a career in sports, a career in music, a career in teaching, nursing, sales, banking, a spouse, a parent, whatever it may be. But when we get to those points in life and the years pass, we still do not see ourselves as elderly people, even though we know we will become just that one day. With that perspective, you just don't relate to them well—unless you are an elderly person. Sometimes they find themselves spending a lot of time

WHAT ARE WE CHASING?

alone as their children go off and make lives of their own. When the elderly look in the mirror, they have so much more to see—they have been through more trials and tribulations. They have grown into a much more comfortable sense of who they are, based mostly on where they have been. The things that used to be important to them no longer are. That is why they get a laugh at our expense when we see them walking around in those silly outfits without a care in the world. They laugh because they know how worried we are about the way we look and how we appear to others around us. They have once felt the same way, and now they have grown to see that as a waste of time. We look just as silly to them as they do to us. They have come to learn that our culture has most of us confused about what is important. They look in the mirror and realize that they have spent too much time on what's not important and choose not to do that anymore.

That does not mean that one person should have the same things be the most important to them as what is the most important to the next person, but the things that have the truest meaning in one's life should be the priority for that person. One person's priorities may be faith, family, career, while another person's may be a specific mission he or she has been called to do. Regardless, nobody's priority would consist of worrying about what anyone else thinks... but we still do it.

The fact is that sometimes it takes a loss of some kind, or a confrontation with hard times, that makes us reassess our priorities. For instance, I am sure we have all heard someone say, "It makes you realize what is really important" after the loss of a friend or a loved one, or after someone in the family becomes ill, maybe after losing a job or wrecking a car, any kind of event that has an enormous effect on us. When people say that, I have to wonder why it takes something like that to realize what is really important. Why can't we realize that every day? Well, I guess that is what happens as we get older. We do start to figure out what's really important.

With age comes wisdom, so they say. I guess there is some truth to that. Think about what advice you could give your younger self when you get older. The pitfalls you could warn your younger self about would help you so much. You could be warned of what decisions you made that were hurtful to yourself and to others, and you would know how much those decisions were not worth it. Most of the hurtful decisions were made out of a desire for instant gratification or pleasure, which will fade shortly thereafter, and take us away from the true happiness that life has to offer us. The thing about it is we already have the wisdom, we just don't have the self-discipline to avoid the instant pleasure that our culture teaches us to go after every minute of every day.

It takes a lifetime of experiences to realize what is really important and to realize it every day. As we get older, we just tend to weed out those things that have such trivial meaning, and we probably wish we would have done it sooner. Looking in the mirror as we get older, we face our mortality. We realize it will all be over one day, and we choose not to waste any more time than necessary. In our younger or middle age years, we run around trying to do more, get more, and see more, chasing everything there is to chase as if we were immortal and will live forever. For what? Then, when we get near the end,

WHAT ARE WE CHASING?

we wonder why we didn't spend more time doing the things that were really important.

Another thing to remember is we really don't know what the plan is or when our mortality will be staring us in the face. We don't have to be old to leave this life. You never know when it is the last time you will be looking in that mirror. You are looking at your mortality every day; the elderly are just more aware of it. The next time you look in the mirror, ask yourself what is really important. Answer yourself honestly and spend the rest of your time chasing those things—the important things. Not what anyone else thinks is important, but the things you know are important.

2

Relationships

THE RELATIONSHIPS WE HAVE are a big factor in determining the direction our lives will take. Whether it is a working relationship, a sibling relationship, a romantic relationship, a relationship between friends, a parent-child relationship, or any relationship we have with anybody during the daily activity of our lives, they all affect us. Any person we have a relationship with has an effect on us and we have an effect on them. Some effects are good, and some are not good. We often do not realize the effect we are having on the other person because we are so in tune with how that relationship is affecting us.

A simple example would be, let's say, in a parent-child relationship.

WHAT ARE WE CHASING?

The parent is constantly telling the child what he or she is doing wrong and why they need to do something better, which is going to have a clear effect on the child. The child is going to feel like no matter what he or she does will not be good enough for the parent. Now if the parent is complimentary and encouraging, the child's response could be increased effort and determination. If the child feels accepted in the relationship, he or she will not feel as if they were walking around on eggshells waiting to do something wrong.

Feeling accepted in a relationship is what makes it a stronger relationship as long as we don't sacrifice who we are in order to be accepted. We need to be accepted for who we are and what we believe. We shouldn't change in order for somebody to accept us. If somebody we have a relationship with does not accept us for who we are, and we try to conform to what we think that person needs from us in order for them to accept us, that relationship will not last.

On the other hand, that means we must do the same for people we are in a relationship with. We must accept people for who they are, where they've been, where they are trying to go, the good, the bad, and everything that goes along with being in a relationship with them. Sounds easy enough, doesn't it? We can do that, can't we? No.

We are human, and instead of accepting people for who they are, we judge them. We just cannot help it. It is one of our biggest weaknesses as humans. We know it's wrong, but we just can't help it. We judge others and others judge us. Maybe that is why we are so worried about what everyone else thinks, because we know people are worrying about what we think.

We are actually more judgmental towards the people we have close relationships with than we are to strangers. We judge our spouse, we judge our kids, we judge our boss, our friends, our siblings, pretty much anybody we deal with on a daily basis. Now we don't wake up in the morning and say, "Let's go around and judge everyone today," but as the day progresses and we face whatever challenges cross our paths that day, and interact with the people we must interact with that day, it just happens. Judging people does not mean you have to say anything either. This could all just be in the committee in your head. You find yourself having thoughts like, *Why did he do that?* or *Why would she wear that?* Think about what teenagers must go through. Do you know how many people are telling them what to do and what not to do? They may get up in the morning to a parent questioning the clothes they are wearing and asking them how they expect to do well in school today if all they are going to eat is half of a cereal bar. Then they get to school and have a teacher explaining to them how the homework they turned in could be much neater, and then after school they go to baseball practice and the coach is telling them how they are doing something all wrong, not to mention how they shouldn't be wearing those kinds of socks on the baseball field. It's no wonder teenagers don't talk to anybody but each other for a few years. The only people they get acceptance from are other teenagers.

In relationships, the people we are most comfortable with are the people we feel accepted by. We are more comfortable being our true selves when someone accepts us just the way we are, with whatever baggage that may come with. We will be much more hesitant to reveal ourselves to people we feel will judge whatever we say or do.

With that in mind, think about the relationships we have where we struggle to accept those people the way they are. We make it harder for them to fully reveal themselves to us. Even your spouse, child, parent, or sibling may not be giving you their true selves for fear of being judged. These aren't some strangers we are dealing with. I am talking about people we love, people closest to us. Sometimes the expectations we have in our minds for those we have the closest relationships with are unrealistic and overwhelming and, quite honestly, are not even expectations we would put on ourselves. Part of our human nature is to try and be in control of situations. One of our biggest fears is to not be in control. In relationships, when someone does not do what we expect of them or they do not handle something the way we may handle it, we get a sense that we have no control over that situation, even though it was not our situation to worry about to begin with.

I'll give you a couple examples.

A husband leaves at 8:00 AM to go to work. On a normal day, his wife will get the kids off to school, do the dishes, straighten up the house, do the laundry, maybe take a trip to the grocery store, and have dinner ready or close to it when he comes home. Now, he can get pretty used to these things being done and may tend to expect that it should always be this way. So one day he comes home, the laundry is in a basket on the couch not folded, there is nothing to drink in the fridge, and his wife is running out to get some takeout food because she didn't have time to cook dinner. His first thought is *What in the world has been going on here all day?* and *What has my wife been doing around here all day?* He may not even say anything about it to his wife, but he is now stewing about that fact that he has been at work all day and she can't even get the housework done. He does not even bother to ask why, he just knows his expectations were not met. He had no control of that situation and he is not comfortable with that. In his head, things just aren't the way they should be. Of course, he has no idea of the obstacles his wife may have faced that day that could have affected what she had originally planned to accomplish.

Well, it just so happens that on this day, she dropped the kids off at school, got home, and realized that one of her children left their lunchbox sitting on the table. Now she can't sit down and do her shopping list because she has to get dressed (she dropped the kids off through the carpool line in her pajamas because everybody was running late, as they are every morning), and she cannot rightly walk the lunchbox into the school in her pajamas. So she got herself together and walked the lunchbox into the school but, on the way out, ran into one of her best friends sobbing in the parking lot because she just found out her mother is ill and may not have long to live. She spent a good hour with her friend consoling her over a cup of coffee and offered to help in any way she can. Turns out the woman needed help with child care for her kids after school that afternoon, so she gladly helped her with that. So when she arrived home it was almost lunchtime, and she realized she hadn't even cleaned up the breakfast dishes yet. She cleaned up a little bit, started a load of laundry and had some lunch and, at that point, it occurred to her that this was the first thing she

WHAT ARE WE CHASING?

had eaten today. Before she knew it it was 2:00 PM, and she had to get back in the car pool line to not only pick up her kids, but her friend's kids too. So now when she got home she had to put together snacks for all these kids which proved to be difficult because, of course, she did not make it to the store as she had originally planned. She threw something together—crackers with peanut butter and a few cups of water—which were protested by her own kids because they like juice but, of course, they were all out. She walked by the laundry room on the way to get some paper for her friend's kids to do their homework, which reminded her to throw the laundry that she started earlier in the dryer. After two of the kids spilled their water on the floor, she cleaned that up and helped one of them who was having trouble with homework, hoping this will be the last thing she will have to do before figuring out what to do for dinner. Finally, around five, her friend called and asked if she could bring her kids home in about thirty minutes. On the way out, luckily passing the laundry room again, she took the laundry out of the dryer, threw it in the basket, and set it on the couch to fold later. She took the kids to her friend's house and got back home about five minutes before her husband walked in the door. He walked in the door and his first thought when he saw the laundry on the couch unfolded, a bunch of cups in the sink, and his wife scurrying to get back out the door to get some dinner is that she had been doing nothing around here all day. He has made an assumption that his wife did not do what she was supposed to do or what he expects she should do just by walking in the door. He hasn't asked her about it and when she tries to talk about her day with him, he is so caught up on how his day went that he really does not want to hear about it. He is so focused on himself, how his day was, and how things weren't the way he thought they should be when he got home that he doesn't want to talk about it.

A lack of communication in any relationship is one of the biggest downfalls there is. He really does not talk about what he is angry about, and she really never talks about the circumstances that made it a tough day for her. The circumstances could just as easily have been reversed. She could have had a perfect day, got everything done she had planned to for that day, and had dinner waiting on her husband when he got home not knowing that as he was about to leave work, his boss stopped and asked him to go over a few more things with him that took about thirty minutes and when he finally got in the car to leave, he started to call his wife to let her know he was running late and realized that his cell phone was dead. As he was driving home, he ran into traffic due to an accident that had him sitting still on the highway. So when he got home an hour and half late, all his wife thought was, *First of all, how is it possible he is an hour late, and how could he not even have called to tell me he would be late, knowing that I am here trying to have everything ready for him by the time he gets home?* She just carried on with the evening, getting her kids showered and ready for bed, and they barely discussed why he was late to begin with.

Lack of communication and having trouble accepting things we don't have control of are huge obstacles in relationships. We can only control our actions, which include our reactions to circumstances that may have been an inconvenience to us but are out of our control. In our relationships, no matter who they are with—a spouse, a child, a parent, or a friend—the times we are away from these people we are having our own experiences, and so are they.

We are each a little different every time we see each other after a period of time apart. There is an opportunity to accept or judge every time we see each other. Your child may leave for school in a great mood in the morning, and for some reason when he comes home he is in a bad mood. Well, he experienced something that day. Now it was easy to accept him this morning when he was in a great mood, but now that he is in a bad mood, we may not feel like dealing with that. We would much rather he be in a good mood, but it is out of our control. Chances are the bad mood will cease quicker if we can be accepting and be there for him, rather than just feeling like he needs to get over it, which may be what we would like to tell him. We want to feel accepted all the time, in whatever state of mind we are in. When we feel accepted we communicate better, and when we communicate better, we have better relationships.

We also must accept the fact that some relationships that we think are great relationships will not last forever. Of course relationships with children, siblings, or parents will, for the most part, last forever. They may not always be good relationships, but they are still relationships. The relationships we have with friends are probably the most interesting. So many people we call friends come in and out of our lives during the different stages of our lives, from the time we are in school, even elementary school, until the time we take our last breath. In third grade, most of us had somebody we called our best friend, and chances are you have no idea where that person is today. You had a relationship, though; you might have played sports together, sat at lunch together, or played on the school playground together. You might have only been eight or nine years old, but even at that age you had an effect on someone, and someone had an effect on you. This kid may have been the one whom you played your first whiffle ball game with, and it may have been that the first time that kid played a video game was at your house. You may have tried broccoli for the first time while eating dinner at this kid's house, even though you would never have tried it at home but you felt like you had to eat it because someone else's mom made it. He or she may have had their first sleepover at your house. In third grade, you did everything with your best friends, and now you don't even know where they are. In fact, by the time you crossed paths in middle school when you were in seventh grade, you barely acknowledged each other and now have not been friends for two years.

In seventh grade we may have had a different best friend that lasted another couple of years. As adults, we may still get fooled into thinking we have a best friend for life. It just does not happen all that often where you will have many best friends for the rest of your life. Friends come in and out of our lives for a variety of different reasons. Usually you met in a period of your lives when you had the same interests, whatever they were. At one point we may have had a best friend whom we liked to go to ballgame or a movie with. We may have had one whom we liked to have a couple of drinks with. We may have been in a stage where we had one whom we had

WHAT ARE WE CHASING?

too many drinks with and maybe experimented with drugs of some kind. Maybe many years later we have no interest in drugs or alcohol, but at the time that was our best friend, and that was what we enjoyed doing together. Maybe one of you still does like to go to ballgames or out for drinks, and maybe one of you does not. People are constantly changing, so we lose the common interests we once had.

When you have a best friend whom you can just spend time doing nothing with, or not always feeling like you have to have a plan, you have a best friend who will last. Someone whom you can be apart from for a year and then just pick up where you left off, someone who has a legitimate interest in you and you in them, regardless if your lives go in different directions—that is a best friend.

The best thing to do with the friends who have come and gone is to remember the times you enjoyed spending with them and learn from the times that being friends with them may have led you down the wrong path. Sometimes we just have to go down the wrong path to get where we are supposed to be. We just have to make sure we learn from it. A relationship with a friend is no different from any other relationship in the sense that we are going to have an effect on them and they will have an effect on us. Sometimes we realize we are different from somebody else and it may be best that we do not remain a friend to them. It is still important to accept them just the way they are as you want them to accept you for who you are.

To not learn from your relationships is a mistake. When we look back on our relationships, we realize there are many things we would do differently. One of the things we struggle to do most in relationships is to forgive. If somebody hurts us in some way, we walk around with a grudge as if they have ruined our life. With our current culture of reality television and social media, we are more worried about looking bad after somebody has hurt us, rather than learning why they hurt us and choosing the road of forgiveness. Forgiveness is a selfless act, which is in conflict with the way our culture is today. Think about how brutal it is in the media when a public figure makes a mistake. We hear and see every detail as they get publicly punished on the airways and the media digs up as much dirt as they can to magnify the mistake.

Now the majority of us have made big mistakes, hurting someone in the process, and I am quite sure we would not want that celebrated on the airways. If we are truly remorseful for our mistake and we are forgiven by the person we hurt, it changes us and humbles us into being a better person based on what we have learned. I am sure there are people in our life that we wish would forgive us for something we may have done to hurt them, so when you realize that, think about the people who wish you would forgive them and how you could change their life by the selfless act of forgiveness. Not only do you change someone else's life when you forgive, you change your own. The more you forgive the more you will grow, and the more you will see the humanness in yourself and others. It is a powerful experience to see conversion of heart in yourself and in others. It is understandably not always easy to forgive, but many relationships would be better off and last longer if forgiveness was part of relationships. People go to their graves not speaking to siblings, friends, parents, children—all because they could not forgive. Don't get caught up in unforgiveness. We are not on this earth long enough to take grudges to the grave.

The last thing we have to do is forgive ourselves. If you are in a relationship with someone and you do something that hurts them, whether they forgive you or not you have to be able to forgive yourself. If you have owned up to whatever it is you have done and are sorry and have shown remorse, there is nothing else you can do. It is over and you have to move on. It may be a regret and something you learned from, and you may think about it from time to time just wishing it never happened, but learn from it, forgive yourself, and move on.

I will say this: life is short, so make your important relationships a priority. Our culture has us believing that being successful and having lots of money and lots of stuff is what's important. In reality, when you are that old man or woman in the grocery store with the funny hat and socks pulled up, do you think you will care so much about all that stuff? Maybe it would be nicer to be surrounded by the people you developed great relationships with, relationships in which you accepted the other for who they are and they accepted you in the same way, relationships where you could spend time together and not feel like something has to be said every second. If you ask me, that is way more important than money or possessions. When we leave this earth we won't have any of our possessions with us, but I believe we will have the opportunity to spend time with the souls of the people we have had great relationships with. Eternity is a long time to miss those possessions that we may have wrongly made so important to us.

If you knew today was your last day here on earth, what would you realize you are going to miss the most? Chances are it would not be what you would miss the most, but who. Make people a priority over material pleasure and wealth. Great relationships help us grow, learn, recover, forgive, experience great joy and experience great sadness, they help us live life to the fullest. They give us the opportunity to experience every emotion possible. Do you want to have things, or do you want to have a life?

3

Parenting

THE PRIVILEGE OF HAVING A CHILD is second to none. It is the single biggest event that takes the focus off ourselves and on to somebody else. The overwhelming unconditional love that fills us when we have a child is something that cannot be felt in any other way. It creates an instant change in us that cannot be duplicated. It comes with emotions we have never faced, feelings we cannot describe, responsibilities we have never had, and immediate expectations of being something we have never been before—a parent. We know when we become a parent we are now responsible for helping another human being become all they are capable of becoming. As parents, we all have different ideas on what we think is best for our children, whether they are babies or whether they are young adults.

WHAT ARE WE CHASING?

It all starts when they are infants. Some parents insist infants should sleep on their stomachs, while others are sure they should sleep on their back. Some say you should get them in a crib as soon as possible, some say if they stay in the bed with you for a while it is fine. We seek the advice of our own parents, friends who have become parents before us, and any so-called expert we see on a daytime talk show. I am not sure what makes some of these people experts, but they sure have a lot of advice for us. I guess we seek this information because becoming a parent for the first time is an unknown journey that we will be on for the rest of our life. We as a culture do not do so well with the unknown. We are in an age where if you want to know how to do something, you just look it up on the computer and have the information immediately. A child does not come with instructions or an immediate website that can give you the exact details on how to raise him or her. We need to take advantage of any support we may have around us that can help us with the transition to becoming a parent, but we will find out that we must quickly learn how to make good decisions.

Any decision we now make affects the life of another which can at times seem overwhelming. Now if you are late for work and lose your job, you have affected your child as well. This child's life will be shaped and formed by the environment created by the parents.

Becoming a parent means learning how to set our own selfish desires aside for the needs of another. Many of us growing up have a huge desire to become a parent, so it is a sacrifice we are more than willing to make. It is not easy by any means, but it doesn't take much more than being in that delivery room to realize the miracle and blessing it is to have a child. Being a parent was, is now, and always will be the most important job we can ever have. We now have someone who is going to look up to us, want to be like us, and want to do everything we do, for better or worse. It doesn't take long to understand what a challenge it will be, not so much just because we have a child, but because of the changes it makes to our own lives.

When the children are babies, we face extreme sleep deprivation, emotional challenges, challenges in our marital relationship and everything that goes along with that. We were once the center of attention from our spouse, and now the child is the center of attention. It is to be expected, but we do not realize how much of an emotional adjustment that may be. It is a small tradeoff for the joy we will receive from being a parent.

The challenges of being parents change as children go from being babies to toddlers, to elementary age, and to the adolescence stages. When they are babies, we have to worry about getting them on a schedule for sleeping and eating, we have to make sure we have a diaper bag, and whatever other bags are necessary when we leave the house for whatever situation that might come up. A diaper blowout in the grocery store could be a disaster if we are not properly prepared. What used to require thirty minutes to get out the door now takes ninety minutes, not to mention that as you are walking out the door, the baby decides this would be the best time to take care of some personal business that requires an immediate express diaper change all the while with bags on our shoulder, coat

WHAT ARE WE CHASING?

on, and keys in our hand. If we were not multitaskers before, we quickly learn how to become one. Bottles, pacifiers, toys, baby books, all for a five-minute ride and a trip to the grocery store or church. We barely even worry about what we have on or what we look like for those first few weeks until we finally get acclimated to the baby's schedule. In this stage, the child is completely dependent on us. We better sleep when they sleep or we will be walking around in a battle for our sanity. During this stage, we learn a lot about ourselves, our spouse, our parents, and anyone else participating in the care of this child.

Emotions will range from the pure joy of just holding the child to pure anguish from lack of sleep. We learn if we have true patience and, if we don't, we must develop it. Our own lives may temporarily be put on hold, although at the time it may not feel temporary. Our communications with other adults are cut in half, leaving us sometimes talking to ourselves. Funny thing about it is that once the child is not a baby anymore and heads into the toddler and elementary stages, a lot of us start talking about having another one. That is what tells us how big a blessing having a child is. All of our time, communications, personal needs, wants, and all of our goals we would willingly sacrifice all over again for another child. We can't help it. We love this baby, and our instincts are to take care of and protect this baby with everything we have. Our baby is not someone we have to get to know to fall in love with. It is instant. It is a powerful realization and understanding that we have the ability to love in this way.

For most of us who are parents, no matter how old our child is they are always our baby. I have heard parents speaking of their forty-year-old child and referring to the child as their baby. The way parents see their children, from the time they are conceived and for the rest of their lives, is different from the way anyone else sees their child. It is an unbreakable bond that exists no matter what happens for the rest of their lives. The baby stage is one that the parents will always remember and will often fall back on throughout the life of the child.

As the child grows into the crawling and toddler stages, we as parents have a whole new set of challenges to deal with. We have to make sure we have plastic covers in all the outlets, safety handles on all the doors and cabinets, and floors must be swept constantly if we do not want our child to taste that nickel that fell on the floor. A paper clip on the floor, or the unfinished dog food, is quite the temptation for our little ones once they are mobile around the house. Every cabinet, drawer, or door that we do not want opened must be bolted in some way or another. Heaven forbid the child opens that cabinet under the sink with all the cleaning supplies. The little things we must be aware of have now increased tremendously. We have to block steps, put up gates, and remove any breakable item within arm's reach of our precious little one. All the while, we must maintain a schedule that coincides with our child, which is virtually impossible if we want to get anything done. But we do our best, we start to have a regular schedule going, and then God has a different plan for some of us—gives us another one. Now we have all these responsibilities and expectations times two.

WHAT ARE WE CHASING?

We just got one child through the baby stage and here comes another. Now we get even less sleep, have even more responsibility, and have two lives totally dependent on us. We are exhausted. We are back to baby bags and pacifiers with one child and we are playing goalie trying to keep our other child from sticking a finger in an electrical outlet (which is supposed to have a cover on it but the child managed to pull it off.)

As I mentioned earlier, my wife and I have been blessed with four children; when we had our last one, our oldest was six. We had a six-year-old, a four-year-old, a fifteen-month-old, and an infant. I truly believe God does not give you more than you can handle. Now that doesn't mean we handle things perfectly all the time, but somehow, some way, we manage. During this time, we had two kids in diapers, three taking naps, one of them was in preschool, and one of them was in kindergarten—it was quite an adventure!

As a parent—and I think most would agree—this time goes by so fast. I have been teaching my fifteen-year-old daughter how to drive and I have a hard time believing it is actually her that I am teaching. I see her being born, learning how to crawl, learning how to walk, walking into her first day of school, singing in her school show, I see her trick or treating, I see her opening Christmas presents, I see her hugging her brothers and sisters, but I don't see her driving, even though I am teaching her.

As we watch our kids go through these stages, we should make a conscious effort to enjoy every minute of it. We know this instinctively, but our culture has us believing that we have to do everything so fast that we forget sometimes to slow down and enjoy the little things, which—if you stop and think about it—aren't really little things at all. Our culture has us believing that if we slow down to enjoy something, we might miss something else.

There are also a lot of things our culture believes our children need that just aren't necessary. Our children do not need the latest name-brand clothes, the latest video games or the newest phones, they do not need iPods or iPads, they do not need an entertainment system in their car for every thirty-minute ride they take, they do not need the newest bike, they do not need the greatest baseball bat, and it is all right if they are the only one on the block without a trampoline. Our children just do not need any of these things from us. The one thing they need from us is our time. Yes, they need us to love them and teach them how to be respectful and all of those things, but they will get none of that if we do not give them our time. They need our time. They need to see us slow down in this fast-paced world, which the culture has led us to believe will run you over if you stop for even a minute to give them our time.

When our children become adults and look back at their childhood, their memories will be of time spent together and not the things they had. Unfortunately, if we do not spend time with them, they will remember that too. I know sometimes we are tired, we may have had a long day at work, we have bills to pay, places we need to go, things that need to be fixed, and sometimes we just don't feel like having a catch with our son or having a tea party with our daughter. Do it anyway. The majority of time, once we get started, we enjoy the time we are spending with our children. We should put everything aside and spend as much time as we can with our children. Watching our children reach milestones gives us more joy than anything we can ever have. I am convinced that we learn more from our children than they do from us.

Nothing reaches our hearts and souls the way watching our children grow does. One day they can't walk and the next day they can. One day they can't read, the next day they can. One day they can't add, the next day they can. We never know when those days are going to be. As they grow, we begin to see their personalities emerge. They get involved in sports, music, clubs at school, they become creative in their own way, and all they want to do is share it all with us.

The experiences my wife and I share with our four children are more important to us than anything we could ever have. They are all so creative, but in such different ways. Our fifteen-year-old daughter has learned to sew and she loves making dresses for her younger cousins. She plays the violin, and to go watch one of her performances amazes me. I wouldn't even know how to hold a violin and my daughter is playing the most beautiful music. She is soft-spoken, patient, and would like to get involved in special education when she is older. How lucky are we as parents to watch a child emerge and begin to realize their own potential? Now my twelve-year-old daughter could not be more different from her sister. She is an animal lover to the extreme, and we would be amazed if her future career does not involve animals. She will make us let a spider out of the house instead of stepping on it and killing it. I cannot begin to tell you all the little critters she has made a home for and had living in her room, sometimes without our knowledge. It pulls at her heart to see anyone or anything suffer. One day when she was about eight, her grandmother bought her a little toy guitar. Now, how is it possible to know that one little thing like that could be a life-changer? My daughter started taking guitar lessons and now, four years later, she does performances and recitals with the poise of an accomplished artist. It's funny because unlike her sister, she is quite impatient, often says things without thinking them through, and concerns herself with many things that are quite irrelevant. Now, we would not want to change her for anything. She is the clown of the family and has the ability to crack up her siblings on a regular basis. It's just amazing—when she is on stage with a microphone in front of her and a guitar in her hand—to see the confidence and joy she can express to the people watching. To listen to this twelve-year-old sing and play so beautifully, and then take in the fact that it is my own daughter—what's more important than that?

Then there is my oldest son who just turned ten. He's the little engineer of the house. Give him something to put together, build, connect, or wire and he will take care of the rest. He will spend two hours figuring out how to get something to work when I would have lost interest in five minutes. You can just see that little motor in his brain working when he is put to the challenge. I have learned from my son that there is more than one way to grow up in a household. When I grew up, I played baseball and football, and I had a bunch of friends who did the same. My son is completely opposite to how I was growing up, and I can't help but be amazed at the things he does. One day he may be an architect or an engineer, or something else that will certainly be like a foreign language to me. I often find myself looking at him in amazement wondering, *How did he do that?* I look forward to seeing what he will become.

Then comes his little brother, fifteen months younger than him and the youngest of the four. He is for sure the energizer of the house. He wakes up, goes about a million miles an hour all day, and then goes to sleep. He wakes up the next day, same thing. A total contradiction to his brother, he loves the outdoors, all sports, and especially loves baseball. How great is it to see your eight-year-old catch his first fly ball after about the first ninety-nine he missed? That is the way he is, though: he will not give up until he can do something. He is also the one we can tell something and he will not forget it. Just watching our kids grow up and work their way into becoming who they will be is priceless. Of course, my wife and I are proud of all these kids and the things they accomplish. Watching them play music, hit home runs, or create something we could not have imagined are all moments to be proud of, but the times that make you the most proud are quite unexpected.

How about your fifteen-year-old who, working as a babysitter all summer, tells you she wants to take the family out to lunch, or your twelve-year-old asking you to take her shopping to spend the money she saved up on her brother for his birthday, or your oldest son who, asking you all summer how he can make some money so he can buy something, finally gets his sister to give him ten bucks for doing some of her chores and he puts in the collection basket at church, which inspires his eight-year-old brother to put money in the basket as well. These are the times we are the proudest of our children. It is not the times they get straight A's or hit home runs, but it is the times that they teach us lessons we have already learned and sometimes forgotten.

We need to soak in all the time we can with our kids, take time to enjoy all the little moments that touch our hearts. There is something about that first time we drop our kids off for the first day of school in kindergarten and they are walking in with a book bag that is bigger than them on their back. They are growing up right in front of our eyes, and there is something special about every milestone they hit. We need to get lost in those moments and cherish them. We need to teach them what they need to become, not what they need to have or do. Being around our children, or any other children for that matter, helps us realize that we too at one time had that innocent, trusting, easygoing approach to each day that totally gets lost in the hustle and bustle of today's culture. I know the more time I spend with my kids the better I feel. I think it is good for the soul.

Raising our kids is certainly a challenge in today's culture, especially as they get into those teenage years. At this stage, one of the most important reasons we need to spend so much time with our kids is because if we don't, our culture will. I know that I am not willing to take that chance. We were all teenagers once, and we all have our memories of questionable decisions and bad choices, but there seems to be so much more pressure on kids today and, along with that, the opportunities to go down the wrong path are way more available to our teenagers today than in years past. It seems that if our teenagers are not

WHAT ARE WE CHASING?

excelling in five different activities, have the best grades, wear the best clothes, look the best, or hang out with the most popular kids, they have no chance. That is what our culture will have them, and sometimes us, believe. We get so focused on getting them to do all they can do rather than letting them become all they can be. Our culture has them believing that to be successful they have to submerge themselves in as many things as they can without leaving a second to spare, sometimes stepping on whatever toes necessary to do so. They get bombarded by television, music, and the internet, all teaching them to do all they can, and get all they can, as fast as they can. The role models they often have today make decisions based on instant pleasure rather than true morality and happiness. There is very little out there that will tell them how to make good decisions, decisions ethically and morally based.

This is where we as parents need to come in. We know what a struggle it is to be in today's culture and, all the while, our teenagers naturally think they know everything and have all the answers. It is a battle, but a battle we have to fight every day. It may take years of telling our teenagers one thing every day to keep them from making a bad one-second decision. Sometimes they will still make that bad decision even if you have gone over it for years, but we have no choice. We must be relentless in our effort to instill the right moral decision-making skills when faced with the challenges our culture presents. We cannot simply make decisions for them; we must teach them to make good decisions, and when they make bad ones, we must be there to pick them up. We need to do all we can to keep the lines of communication open, be able and willing to talk about the tough issues and circumstances they are going through. We must let them know constantly that they can talk to us about anything, no matter what kind of situation they have gotten themselves into.

It is easy when our kid is getting all A's, doing great in sports and extracurricular activities, staying out of trouble, and making good decisions on who they surround themselves with, but when they run into those tough times, we must be ready to face them head on. As parents, we must be prepared to suffer many times of anguish and stress related to decisions our kids have made. Tough situations don't just go away, and we must not kid ourselves into believing that our kids wouldn't make a bad decision. Being proud of our kids must not be confused with thinking they can do no wrong. Our human nature wants to believe that but we must be realistic, and when the storms of our children come our way, we better have strong roots and be prepared for them. If we knew a hurricane was coming our way, we would get prepared for that. With the culture our kids are faced with today, as much as we do not want to believe it, the storms of our children are coming. Our kids are more desensitized to the implications of doing drugs, drinking alcohol, being sexually active, or most any other thing we would rather they stay away from. Just because it seems like they may not be listening to us, we must still talk to them constantly.

In some respects, our kids may have it better than we did growing up, but the morality of our culture makes it harder for them to make good decisions.

WHAT ARE WE CHASING?

The best thing we can do for our kids is to live a life of virtue and be an example of the true good in the world—not what our culture would have you believe. We need to live this kind of life and then make sure we have the time for them whenever they need us. We need to live a life that makes them see us as a role model, as opposed to what they see and hear in today's culture. We need to help them discover what really is important—a life of virtue, good morals, faith, self-discipline, selflessness, service to others. It is pretty simple stuff. Is it easy? No, it's not always easy, but for the most part our kids know just like we do if we are doing the right thing or not. Sometimes we are, sometimes we aren't, and when we are not doing the right thing, we need to catch ourselves as soon as possible and do the next right thing, teaching our kids to do the same.

Our kids mean more to us than anything in the world, but sometimes we get worn down and tired, finding it hard to fight every single battle to help show them how to lead themselves down the right path. Sometimes we do have to let them fall so they learn how to get back up. They do grow up and lead lives of their own, and what they have learned on the way there, especially from us, will have a lot to do with who they become.

As parents, I think it is more important to nurture who they become as opposed to what they become or what they have. My oldest is only fifteen, but I can imagine I would get more happiness and be more proud of watching her grow into a caring, giving person who does not answer to the influence of today's self-centered culture than if she were to become a millionaire... but that's just me.

4

Money

WHY IS IT THAT OUR CULTURE places such emphasis on money? How much we have, how much we make, how much we spend, is the dollar up, is the dollar down. When I was twenty-one years old, I had been working for a company for about three years and was given a promotion to a managerial position. It was quite an accomplishment in my own mind, knowing that half of the people I went to high school with were in their third year of college and, like most college kids, probably still had very little idea what they were going to do when they got out.

Another reason it felt like a great accomplishment was the fact that I received plenty of criticism when I decided to drop out of college after just three days. I received criticism from friends, my girlfriend, parents, parents of friends, former

WHAT ARE WE CHASING?

teachers, etc. I can remember them all looking at me as if I had lost my mind, a look as if I could never do anything with my life if I didn't go to college.

This is another one of our cultural misconceptions. If only these people realized how many people in our world actually went to college. Not near as many as we think! Don't get me wrong: I think college is a great opportunity for many young people to strive to achieve goals they have set for themselves, and hopefully not goals others have set for them.

When I did drop out of college, I will admit that I had no idea what I was going to do, but I had friends who graduated college and they felt the same way. Our culture would lead you to believe that college is the best way to go, which may be true for many people, but it is likely fewer people than we realize. If I have ten friends who graduated college, I would say about seven of them have jobs or careers that have nothing to do with the degree they graduated with, and five of them have jobs or careers that don't even require a college degree.

Anyway, at the time, this promotion seemed like one of the best things that could happen to me. I enjoyed the success and I took pride in the fact that I would be making a good chunk of cash at such an early age.

Pride is a tricky thing though. A lot of my motivation for having success and making money was for the wrong reasons. I can remember feeling like I could not wait to show all those people who doubted me how I was doing. I began to feel so self-important. After all, our culture teaches us that if we have more money or make more money, we are more important. Of course, not everybody feels that way, and that idea is the farthest thing from the truth. As a parent, I will do all I can to make sure my children do not get that idea, but our culture will give me a run for my money.

I know that as a twenty-one-year-old I was fooled. I wanted to wear the nicest clothes, go to the best places, drive around in a new car, and I wanted to be seen doing all of it. I think as a young person in today's culture, it is harder now to avoid the barrage of information that leads us to believe how important it is to have money. Television, the internet, social media, etc., are all filled with information glorifying the lives of people who make a lot of money. We know more about the lives now of athletes, music stars, movie stars, etc. than ever before. We see their cars, their houses, and we can follow them on social media. It is hard to imagine that it would not have an effect on the younger people in our culture. They get to believing that these things are important, and that having a lot of money will be a problem solver to any issue they may have. Our culture is teaching our kids that if you do not have money, you are not successful. Nothing could be further from the truth.

Another problem with putting so much emphasis on making or having money is that once you start living a certain lifestyle that requires a lot of money, it is so hard for you to go back to less if something were to happen and you were not making that amount of money anymore. People feel shamed if they have to sell their house or their car, so they do all they can to hang on as long as they can even if they really can't afford it.

A good friend of mine was recently telling me about a friend of hers whom she grew up with. Her friend made a name for herself in television and had a great period of phenomenal

WHAT ARE WE CHASING?

success. She could buy what she wanted, drive what she wanted, wear what she wanted, and she did. Unfortunately, her friend ran into some hard times and some things changed. It got to the point where money was going out faster than it came in. She was talking to her friend one day about what she could do to try and balance out this problem a little bit, and she mentioned to her friend that maybe she did not have to drive that particular eighty-thousand-dollar car she had and she could drive something more along the lines of what my friend was driving, which was something more in the twenty-thousand-dollar range. Her friend then explained to her that she could never drive something like that. Now I have to wonder, what does that mean? This person is not a couple of hundred dollars in debt but hundreds of thousands, yet cannot perish the thought of driving a twenty-thousand-dollar car. It's not like she told her to drive a two-hundred-thousand-mile, twenty-year-old car, which probably would have been a better idea.

At what point does what we have, wear, or drive determine who we are? Clearly, this person is equating who she is with how she appears to others. Our culture is filled with people who have tied their happiness to money and possessions because that's what they see and hear all the time. At what point did a lifestyle become more important than a life? Having enough money to have our basic needs met and maybe a little more so we can enjoy our lives seems to be a thing of the past. We go in debt now not for the things we need but for the things we want. In our culture today, it appears to me that the meaning of the word "need" has a different meaning than it has had in the past. I remember growing up and my friends telling me their mom or dad "needed" to get a second job so they would have enough to buy some winter clothes or fix their car. Now, I hear people saying they "need" to get the new iPhone or they "need" to get this new forty-thousand-dollar car. Not only that, but now we have people telling us that we "need" to do these things as well. Haven't you ever had someone tell you, "Oh, man, you need to get this new smartphone," or "You need to buy this or that"? The thing about it is that I would guess that over half of the people buying these things really don't need them and shouldn't be buying them at all. Now, they have to pay for it for two years.

It used to be that if you wanted something, you would save your money for some time and buy it. As parents, we have such a battle in today's culture to teach that to our children. Everybody has to have it, whatever it is, and they have to have it *right now*. If you were to step back and look at everything you have and what you really needed every day, a lot of us have too much. What we need has been distorted by what our culture tells us we need. The one thing our culture will not tell us is that it really could care less about us whatsoever. We can choose to get on the treadmill this culture puts us on and try to keep up with it, but once you get off it, the culture will spit you out like you were never there. It doesn't care about you, your family, what you carry around in your heart, in your mind, or in your soul, but many of us will still try to keep up with it.

Unfortunately for many of us, it will take until we are much older before we realize that what our culture is selling

WHAT ARE WE CHASING?

is not worth the price. As we get older, we realize that all the things we have been chasing really don't mean that much after all. We are mortal and one day we will not be here. As we get older, the realization that money and possessions are not going to miss us really begins to sink in. Sometimes, there is just a feeling that our culture is running around like a loose cannon ready to explode at any minute. The feeling that we should do whatever is necessary to get ahead or have more, no matter what it takes or who we step on along the way, seems more the norm these days than trying to do the right thing.

We put so much on our financial plate that when we have a quiet moment, which is hard to come by in today's culture, we spend that time worrying and stressing about money. Our culture is so busy and consumed with how quickly to get on to the next thing that we have trouble enjoying the moment we are in. During a walk in the park, we are so worried about how we have overloaded our financial plate and overextended our time to unnecessary things that we no longer recognize the smell of the flowers we just walked past, the birds flying above our heads, or our own kids playing on the playground. If we do stop to watch our kids play, within seconds we distract ourselves by looking at our phone, or thinking of the next thing we have to do.

Our culture has filled us with so much noise and distraction that we have trouble just sitting quietly. We fill our houses, our lives, and our time with things we just don't really need, and then we can't get enough of what we don't need. We can't get enough of the things we really don't need. Money and possessions do not satisfy us. They will give us a feeling of pleasure for short periods of time, but then we tend to be unsatisfied or start wanting more or even something else.

Think about that feeling you get when you go out and buy something new. A new shirt, new shoes, new car, or whatever it may be—when we first get it, we think it's the greatest thing ever. How many times do we wear that new shirt before that feeling wears off? Maybe three or four times? How many times do we wear those shoes before we feel like they don't go with this outfit or anything else we have? How long do we drive that new car before that feeling of excitement goes away? Six months maybe, a year at the most? Is that what a twenty, thirty, or forty-thousand-dollar car gets us—a year of pleasure? That's why some of us go and do it all over again in two years, so we can have that feeling once more.

The truth is that if we were to possess more self-discipline with our money and restrain from those purchases that give us momentary pleasure, we would have a much deeper rooted happiness. I will give you some examples of what we can do with our money that will give us true happiness, as opposed to momentary pleasure. These examples will help us slow down and see things a little differently than our culture teaches us to see things, and they will be a lot cheaper than that new car or those new clothes. We might even be able to change some lives and some outlooks along the way.

One afternoon, a man wearing a ball cap comes inside a local pizza restaurant to have lunch. Rather than pulling out his phone and being enamored with the most recent posts on his social media page, he is eating his lunch and people watching, and having an awareness of what is going on around him. In

WHAT ARE WE CHASING?

one corner, there is a baby in a high chair screaming its head off; in a booth are two ladies gossiping about the neighborhood they live in; on the other side are four businessmen in suits all staring down at their phones without speaking a word; and an employee behind the counter is texting someone while a customer is trying to pay their check. As the man in the ball cap continues to eat his lunch, another man in a red shirt walks in by himself and sits down right by the door. As several minutes go by, the man in the ball cap can see that the man in the red shirt is becoming increasingly frustrated that a server has not come over to help him yet. He is actually mumbling to himself, almost loud enough for someone to hear him, because it is taking so long. As he is on the verge of leaving, a server finally comes over and takes his order. The man is cordial as the waitress kindly takes his order. It is clear though to the man in the ball cap that the man in the red shirt still seems aggravated. Aggravated or not, the man in the red shirt seems to be enjoying his lunch, even though in his mind it took some time to get it. As the man fiddles with his phone and continues to show signs of agitation, the waitress checks on him a few times, refills his glass of tea, and at the customer's request, starts to bring him the check.

The man in the ball cap has observed the man in the red shirt during his entire lunch. The man in the cap, after thinking about it a while, determines that it really did not even take that long for the man in the red shirt to get service to begin with. The man in the cap just wonders why this man in the red shirt was having a bad day, or why he was troubled. As he thinks about it some more, the man in the cap gets his check and is getting ready to go. Before he leaves, he calls his waitress over before she gives the other man his check, and asks her for a pen. The waitress kindly hands him a pen and heads over to one of her other tables. The man in the ball cap looks at his check, which comes to about eight dollars. He flips over the check, picks up the pen, and writes, "This is a random act of kindness. Please cover the check of the man in the red shirt by the door and keep the change for yourself." With that, he leaves thirty-five dollars and walks out the door before the waitress comes back or the man in the red shirt can see him.

Now, the man in the red shirt had his eight or ten dollar bill covered, and the waitress got almost a twenty-dollar tip. The new path that day for these two people was set in motion by one extremely simple act of kindness. A man saw another man in distress for whatever reason, and could not help but try to change the course of that man's day. He will likely never see that man again. Spending those thirty-five dollars was certainly not like buying that new car or those new shirts, but spending that money on that day will be something that man in the cap will always be happy about.

Like I said before, the excitement of that new car smell will wear off and those new clothes will shrink and get old, but that man can walk in that pizza place any time over the next twenty years and always feel happy about that thirty-five dollars he spent that day when he just wanted to reach out to a couple of everyday people. Now that's how to spend money and gain happiness. He didn't even break the bank, and now there are two more people who have been affected by a total stranger.

WHAT ARE WE CHASING?

Making a difference in the lives of others is a much surer way to happiness than material possessions. The secondary effect of this act could also be substantial. As it turns out, the waitress is a single mom with two jobs and was hoping to make enough in tips that day to get her son a new jacket because his zipper tore off the day before, and the upcoming weather forecast was filled with temperatures that would require a jacket.

Meanwhile, the man in the red shirt (whose outlook has not been very positive lately) was actually inspired to look at himself in the mirror and see how he had been treating people lately—strangers, coworkers, his wife, and his children. He got to thinking about how short and impatient he had become with people, and he began to think about what he could do to change his behavior. All of this just because of that man in the cap. It was a very small gesture, but it clearly had an effect on these two people.

Sometimes we make the mistake thinking that we have to do something big to help people, especially when it comes to money. The fact is that the smallest gestures can have the biggest effect. We get so overwhelmed by the fact that it will take so much to help so many that we end up doing nothing at all. A small gesture like this one by the man in the cap helped a single mom get a jacket for her son, and helped a man to step back and take a look at his self and what direction his life was going. This kind of gesture is no less of gesture than a millionaire making a big donation to a great cause, but it just won't be on CNN.

Because of this gesture, the two people who benefited from it will likely never forget it either. They too will now be inclined to offer a similar gesture or random act of kindness somewhere down the road. The other great thing about the gesture is that the man in the cap didn't want to be seen or feel any need to be noticed. He was just moved for some reason, at that moment, to make that kind gesture. Sometimes when we do help out in some form, we have the human tendency of wanting to be noticed or recognized for what we have done. The truth is we experience true happiness out of selfless acts. We don't need reassurance or a pat on the back. We know what we did. We can look in the mirror and feel good about doing something for somebody else. It's that simple! The more times we do things like this, the more times we want to do things like this.

Spending a few dollars to make a difference for somebody else will bring more lasting happiness than that new car or new shoes ever will. I do know this: all those things I bought when I first started making money I don't remember much about. The fancy brand-name clothes I bought I don't remember what they even looked like, or the cars I drove I barely remember what they rode like, or the people I spent a lot of that money with just to prove I had it I might remember one or two of their names. It just seems as if we would all do a lot better with money, and make better decisions involving money, if we just didn't worry about how much money others think we have.

I look back on how foolishly I use to act with money and I have to laugh, but in reality it is quite sad. We seem to fall for all the traps our culture sets for us. Our culture tells us that our value is based on what we have, and the fact is that nothing is farther from the truth. There are people out there who have a

WHAT ARE WE CHASING?

family, a roof over their head, a car to drive and plenty of food, but they are still not happy. They want more. They want more money, a bigger house, a nicer car, a boat like the neighbor has. They are just not happy. They don't need any of this stuff, but for some reason they cannot get enough of it. All the while, we have the homeless walking around wishing they had any kind of roof over their head, and we have people who, while walking to work, would be glad to have any vehicle that runs to drive to work. We have people who will be happy if they just have enough to pay their power bill. Sometimes it is very hard to do, but if we could all see things through the eyes of another, our priorities may have a different look.

I know the importance of money or material things in one's mind can change. I look at what I have now and I consider it to be too much or more than I need—but if I had twenty years ago what I have now, I would have still wanted more. Money and the things I could accumulate, or things I could do, used to be very important to me, but now not so much. Everybody's circumstances are different, and financial struggles can be a true burden on a person or a family, but sometimes we have put ourselves in that position.

Our culture convinces us what the latest and greatest thing to spend our money on is what we need, and sometimes we fall for the trap. We stretch ourselves out financially listening to the culture and spending that money on what we don't need. We hear it all the time from our culture, our friends, our family, and our coworkers. People are telling us constantly that we need to buy the latest and greatest thing, or we need to vacation in this certain spot, or we need to try this great restaurant. But really we don't need to do any of that, especially if it will create a financial burden.

We need less. We need to simplify. In time, we will be happier for it. I don't know where we draw the line. It is a fine line—we like to have nice things for ourselves and for our family, but how much is too much? We tend to work harder so we can make more money so we can get more stuff. What if we worked harder on our relationships? What if we worked harder on understanding the basic needs of others? What if we worked harder at not being so self-absorbed? What if we worked harder at not being so focused on what we want? I think it is fair to say that we can work harder on a lot of things that can make much more of a difference in our lives and in our happiness rather than working so hard to accumulate wealth and material possessions. If we spent our time and energy working harder to be a better spouse, a better friend, a better parent, or just an overall better person, isn't that worth more than all those material things we get so hung up on?

We hear people say that money is not that important, but that is another one of those things that we hear or say and, if we are being honest, do not live by. It is important that we have a better awareness not so much of *what we have around us but maybe who we have around us.* We all get to decide for ourselves the things that are really important. So I guess we just have to ask ourselves, what's really important?

5

Faith

OUR CULTURE IS NOT VERY FAVORABLE on having a strong faith life. To have a life filled with faith and spirituality requires time and intentional commitment. The problem in our culture today is that we have so many things taking up our time that we barely have time to breathe.

It comes down to priorities. In a culture that has taken on the attitude of self-promotion and self-interest, faith and spirituality have fallen to the bottom of the priority list. It is very easy today for even someone once filled with faith to get lost in the craziness and busyness our culture confronts us with. The other thing about faith is that the spectrum of possibilities for one's faith is so wide. I know people with no faith at all, and I know people whose faith could not be wavered no matter what happened to them. I would consider myself a person of strong faith, although I have a long way to go in

WHAT ARE WE CHASING?

my faith journey. I am a devout Catholic, and over the past several years I have had tremendous growth in my faith for a variety of different reasons. As I step back and see the different levels of faith in my circle of family and friends, I can begin to see some of the differences in how each of them would handle different situations. I also understand why people who struggle with their faith do some of the things they do, because there was a time when I put very little time and energy into my faith. I went from being pretty disengaged in my faith to being highly engaged—mind you it has been over the course of about twenty-five years, so it does not happen overnight. It is a gradual process, a journey as it is so often called.

In this culture of material possessions, bigger houses, fancier cars, and with more access to seeing and touching all of these things, we get easily distracted from a life of faith because we cannot see and touch it. Faith is unknown, a mystery, and, once mesmerized by the desires of everything we see in our culture, it is hard to trust what we cannot see. When we look at it that way, it makes sense that so many people struggle with it.

I will say this: it seems to me that the loose cannon that our culture has become coincidentally falls at a time when people have put faith on the bottom of the priority list. To struggle with our faith is one thing, but to not give it the time of day is another—that is what our culture leads us to. I know when I got out of high school the last thing on my mind was God, faith, church, or anything similar. That was almost thirty years ago, and today it is enormously harder for a young adult to go out in today's culture, which is built on individualistic accomplishments and achievements, and live a life of great faith. It is by no means impossible, but the challenges today are bigger and more dangerous than ever.

To live a life of faith, we have to be selfless. We have to put others first and put aside our material wants and desires. Unfortunately, our culture teaches us the opposite. It teaches us to get everything we can, any way we can, as quick as we can. If someone were to individually ask us if we wanted to live a deep, meaningful life, or live a shallow life, our normal response would be to say we would want to live a deep, meaningful life. Unfortunately, the majority of what we watch, read, or listen to leads to shallow and selfish thinking. The best way to live a deep and meaningful life is to be completely countercultural. It is also the way to live a life of great faith and true happiness.

To live a life of great faith, we must be willing to be different. We must be willing to show our true selves no matter what the cost. We must be willing to accept the opinions and choices of others even if we do not agree with them. It is best for us to realize that what we think is not always right, and we may not agree with the way someone else may think, but that's all right. To live a life of faith is to do the next right thing as many times a day as we can.

As we make decisions in our lives, we know when we are veering off track or when we are struggling to do the right thing. We buy into the culture's way and we chase things we don't need. We put ourselves ahead of others, and we want to look and act a certain way just so we feel like we fit in. When we do catch ourselves and begin to realize that all we are doing and all that we are chasing is unnecessary, we can focus on doing the next right thing, whatever that might be. The next

WHAT ARE WE CHASING?

right thing might be saying something kind to a loved one whom we have been hard on lately, taking a break from house work and playing a game with our child, letting that car behind us who's in such a hurry get in front of us, or realizing that someone who has not been kind to us is struggling with their own circumstances and we need to accept them for wherever they are in their life journey right now.

We are all broken in one way or another, and a journey in faith helps us to accept who we are, which in turn helps us to be more accepting of others. I can tell you from experience that living a life chasing a journey in faith is more peaceful than chasing what our culture teaches us to chase. The peace that comes with living a humble and simple life is worth more than anything our culture can offer. If and when we do decide to pursue a life rooted in faith, we are more in tune to what it is in our hearts and minds and what we need for true happiness. We are able to sit back and spend some time in total silence, listening to the voice of God in our lives. We generally have so much noise in our lives that we never have time to sit quietly and reflect on what is actually going on in our lives and in the depths of our hearts. If we get the rare opportunity to sit in silence, our first tendency is to check our phone, or turn on the computer or television. Are we that uncomfortable with ourselves that we can't sit in complete silence? It is kind of like when you are on a bad date and neither person knows what to say, and you end up with this gut-wrenching silence. You would think on our own we could sit in silence, but the truth is it is hard for us. It is also true that anytime we feel a bit uncomfortable with a situation, our first reaction is to change the situation, as opposed to trying to deal with why we are uncomfortable.

Quite honestly, that sums up why we struggle so much with faith. To live a life of great faith requires us to get comfortable with being uncomfortable. It requires stepping into something when you really don't know what you are stepping into. I used to be a noise junkie myself. Very rarely was I in my house without the television on, probably watching the same sports highlight show for the fifth time or having some tunes cranked up, mostly the classic rock eighties' tunes of my era. I never sat in silence, and most of us never do. We actually think we need the noise when, in reality, it is quite the opposite. The noise sometimes masks the thoughts and feelings we have in the depths of our hearts and minds. These are sometimes the thoughts and feelings we fear, or would rather not confront on a daily basis. We all have our own inner struggles that are hard to face or admit, and it is sometimes easier to mask those struggles with all the noise we tend to fill our lives with, rather than face them every day. The truth is when we are able to spend time in silence, look to our faith, and listen to the voice of God, facing the inner struggles we have becomes possible. We get to know our own selves better, and we become more realistic with what we expect out of ourselves and out of others. We get more comfortable with the fact that we have flaws, and we become more accepting and comfortable with ourselves the way we are.

The other great effect from this is that we begin to present our true selves to others in a way we have never done before. It will no longer bother us for people to see a flaw in us,

WHAT ARE WE CHASING?

because we have already accepted the fact that we have that flaw. We become more human to others, more humble, more approachable, and we find that we become more patient even with the people we have had trouble being patient with. From experience, I can tell you these are some of the things that changed in my world, and it is directly related to digging into my world of faith, spending that time in silence, and listening to the voice of God.

The best thing about growing in your faith is that we begin to take the focus off ourselves. When we are lacking or struggling in our faith, we are so self-interested and self-focused that we fail to see so much of what is going on around us. We struggle to see what is going on in the lives of our family and closest friends. Of course, we know what they are doing every day and we are still spending time with them, but we have no connection to what it is that is important to them or what struggles they are having. We get caught up in a culture that teaches us to only do things for or with somebody if it has a benefit for us, when, quite honestly, true happiness comes from doing the exact opposite.

As we grow in our faith, we become genuine to ourselves and to others. We develop true care and concern for those around us, sometimes overlooking our own wants or needs. And, even better than that, we don't mind doing it. We begin to find that true happiness comes from serving others. We start to look for ways we can do something for somebody else without any expectations. We begin to live in a place of true peace because we realize that all of the things we thought we needed are really not all that important.

Faith, God, heaven, and hell are things we either believe in or we don't, but the reality is even if we do believe in these things, many of us live as if we don't. If we truly believe there is a God and that there is a heaven and hell, how is it that our culture can convince so many of us to live as if none of this is true, or that we can pretty much live however we want and we will still end up in Heaven?

We place such emphasis on earthly possessions that we forget how much they really do not matter. We are born into this world with the same thing we take out of it—nothing. We place such emphasis on the time we are here, but that time pales in comparison to the time we are not here.

If you took a plain piece of white paper and a pencil and just put a small dot right in the middle of that piece of paper, you would barely even see the dot on the paper because it is such a small part of it. It is kind of like our time here on earth. That dot represents the time we are here, while the rest of the paper represents eternity and the time we are not here. So it makes me wonder why, in this day and age with all of our advanced technology and great resources, do we focus so much on that little dot, which, in comparison to the rest of the piece of paper, is such an insignificant amount of time? Not insignificant in the sense of what we do with the time we are here, but it is really just a drop in a bucket as far as time is concerned.

In most other areas of our life, we would put our focus on the whole piece of paper as opposed to the dot. Let's say that dot represented us getting one million dollars one time, but the rest of the piece of paper represented us getting two

WHAT ARE WE CHASING?

hundred fifty thousand dollars a year for the rest of our life. What would we focus on? In other areas of our life, we can see the big picture and focus on what is more relevant, but when it comes to the importance of faith being a real priority in our life, we have trouble seeing the relevance.

It is hard, there is no doubt about that. As busy as we have made ourselves these days, we live day to day and sometimes even minute to minute. Our human nature tells us to just get through the next thing and, in doing this, we can only see what is directly in front of us. To even bother to worry about something as far off as eternity is something that the culture has no time for. We are too busy. It is just not on the forefront of our minds.

Imagine you are standing directly in front of tremendous oak tree, so close that your nose is practically touching the tree. What would you see? Well, pretty much the only thing you can see is a piece of the trunk of that tree. Now if you take ten steps backwards, what can you see? Maybe you can see the whole tree with all the branches and leaves. Take ten more steps backwards and maybe you can see a few trees, ten more steps back and even more trees. Eventually, you may be able to see the whole forest. Step back some more and you will be able to see the sky, the clouds, and the sun over the forest. Some more steps back and you may be able to see the mountains behind the forest. The more we step back, the more we can see.

It is so easy for us to focus only on what is directly in front of us, and a lot of times we miss out on opportunities because of that. Growing in faith can help us see the forest through the trees. It can help us see ourselves for who we really are.

We are able to accept the parts of us that are broken, and we are able to accept the parts of other people that are broken. While living a life filled with faith, we are more likely to put ourselves in someone else's shoes before we make any kind of determination about the way they are or the things they do.

Growing in faith gives us the determination to fight the urge to be judgmental and the urge to speak loosely about things we shouldn't. We will look out for people, as opposed to trying to be better than them. In fact, we begin to realize that what we do or what we have has no relevance on who we become. We realize that we are better than nobody, and nobody is better than us. We focus on being humble and living with a purpose. Not the purpose that our culture teaches us to live with, but a purpose that encourages us to make a difference in the lives of others, and to help the people around us live the same way. Our time here on earth becomes a life filled with peace, love, hope, and joy, and less about stress, money, possessions, and self-gratification. We realize that we do not need something happening every second of every day, and we do not need everything that everybody else has.

Furthermore, we can become truly happy for those who do have more than us instead of being envious. We actually may begin to focus on what others want and what their dreams are as opposed to our own dreams, and we find ourselves doing all we can to help others achieve their dreams. We find ourselves looking for ways to help those who are struggling, and we realize that many times we can help by doing very small things. All we have to do is be willing to look outside of ourselves.

WHAT ARE WE CHASING?

Living a life of faith helps us to grow in generosity and compassion. We are able to accept others no matter where they may be in this life's journey. We understand that the opinions of others, although often not the same as ours, are important to them, and we respect that. We become aware of the fact that the way we may see something is not the way everybody else sees something and that doesn't make anybody right or wrong. We realize that people's opinions all come from their own life's experiences, and we realize that we are all traveling on our own journey with the information we have taken in during our lifetime.

The thing that changes as we grow in our faith is the information we choose to take in. What we read, what we see, what we watch, and where we go are all more carefully considered as we become more aware of the influential possibilities of everything we take in. We choose to take in things that make us better and make us want to grow in our faith, and we choose to resist the things that lead us away from faith and towards self-gratification. Our journey is always headed towards something, which also means it is headed away from something. A journey towards a stronger life in faith helps to lead us away from the things that stop us from being the best person we can be. In order to succeed in this journey, we must be willing to turn off the chaos and noise we have in our daily lives, even if only for a few moments a day. We must have a self-awareness and possession of ourselves, so we can step away from the noise no matter how important we think it is. The noise will always be there when we get back, believe me, but having the ability to step away and not let it determine the path of our lives is a big part of growing in a life of faith. We learn that it's okay to get away from things for a while, put some work down for a minute, or leave the housework for a while. I try on a daily basis to spend some time in silence, letting my thoughts recharge and reorganize. I began to realize that I got more things accomplished by taking some time to myself than when I just did something nonstop. It seems like our culture has everyone running around as if their hair were on fire. If someone asked us if we would like to slow down for a minute and take a break from the race it seems our life is in sometimes, it would seem like most of us would be glad to take that break. So why don't we? What are we so busy doing, and what makes us think that what we are doing is so important that we just can't slow down for a minute? The answer to that is nothing.

We convince ourselves that most of the things we are doing are important, but what would happen if we weren't doing these things anymore? Chances are most of these things somebody else could do just as well, and things would go on whether we are doing them or not. If we don't take time in silence, the things that keep us so busy will define us, and what we do will become more important than what we become.

Time in silence helps us to recognize and assess our priorities, and helps us relinquish the control we feel we need to have over everything. The fact is we really don't have control over anything or anybody, and the one thing we can work on controlling is ourselves and our reactions.

If we can get into the habit of taking some time out in silence, the next step to a life of great faith is prayer. I'm not talking about praying with family before we eat a meal, or night

WHAT ARE WE CHASING?

time prayer with the kids before bed. That is all important, but I am talking about taking those moments of silence and spending a few minutes a day in personal prayer. Taking a few minutes a day in personal prayer is one sure way to grow in your faith. It is the greatest habit to help us see who we really are, what we really struggle with, and what we are capable of becoming. It allows God to get into the middle of our lives every day, which is just where God wants to be. We do have to turn to Him. God is constantly there just waiting for us to turn to Him, but so often we don't. He will still be there the next day, and the day after that, and every day until the day we are no longer here, just waiting for us to turn to Him. I have gotten in the habit of spending ten minutes a day in personal prayer, and I have learned that it is the ultimate way to turn to God and change your faith life.

For those of us who do have children, we can think about how much we want for our kids and how we would do anything for them. My two boys at the ages of nine and ten look to me as if I know everything. They think if there is something they don't know, they can just ask Dad and he'll know. When my girls were a little younger, they looked at their mom the same way. Until they reach a certain age or point in their life, they have no idea how imperfect and broken we all really are. Think about how often our children turn to us, and part of us is just hoping we are doing the right thing for them no matter what it is.

We make decisions for our children with the best of intentions, and because we think that decision will be the best thing for them. Generally, we know what is better for our kids than they do, mainly because of our own experiences, so we make our decisions based on that information. Children are much more apt to turn to someone when they have a problem or don't have the answer to something, but as adults, we often feel as if we have nowhere to turn. There is nothing farther from the truth. Whatever storms come our way during the course of our life, we can always turn to God. Ten minutes a day in prayer is a habit that will help you through the storms we encounter, and help you prepare for the storms that are to come. It will also help us when we have a struggle in life and we are the cause of a storm that affects others. If our kids can turn to us with all of our faults and brokenness, why wouldn't we turn to God when we need answers in our own lives? When we begin to do that on a regular basis, we will get the answers we need—maybe not the answers we want, but the answers we need.

Just like our children, we often do not even know what is best for ourselves, and since God is there waiting for us anyway, why not turn to Him? No matter where we are in our spiritual journey, God is there waiting for us to turn to Him. Even if we have not really started our journey, or had any kind of relationship with God whatsoever, we can still turn to Him today and He will be there. It is never too late, and God does not have any favorites. Many times it takes people until they are in their fifties or sixties to turn to God and start a relationship with Him.

It takes us seeing our own mortality to realize how irrelevant some of the things we used to hold in such high regard really are. It is hard to live a life of great faith, especially in today's culture, which is one of the simplest reasons we struggle with it. It requires discipline, self-control, a humble demeanor, and a willingness to accept what others will think of you no matter what that may be. It is not easy, but then again most things worth attaining are not easy.

If you want to lose a few pounds, it is not easy, but it is worth it when we do. If we want to get a promotion, we have to work harder, but it is worth that hard work when we get that promotion. If we want to be in a marriage that will last a lifetime, it takes hard work, sacrifice, and acceptance, but it is worth it in the end. If any of these things were easy, everyone would do them. But they are not, and a life of faith is the same way. It is hard to be disciplined, it is hard to accept that there are many things we can't control, it is hard to not envy or covet the material things that everyone else has, it is hard to accept our loved ones just the way they are, and it is hard to accept ourselves just the way we are.

Living a life of great faith is hard, but just like losing those few pounds, getting that promotion, or being in a marriage that lasts a lifetime, it is possible once we commit to it. If we can get to that point in our life of faith, we will realize that it is worth the hard work it takes to get there. When we do get there, it's just as hard to stay there because the temptations of life will keep coming at us. Just like it's hard to keep that weight off and it's hard to keep up with the harder job you have been promoted to, we realize that it is a lifetime commitment to maintain that life of faith. We will fail sometimes, just like we may revert to bad eating habits, just like we may get lazy on the job, and just like we may take our loved ones for granted, but when we know that it is a lifetime commitment, those moments of failures and struggles become bearable.

We realize that our human tendencies will sometimes lead us to places we did not intend to be, but a commitment to a life of faith is like winning the war, even though we know that we will lose a few battles. The fruits of living a committed life of faith will begin to shine through, and our hearts become full of the things that are really important. When we do spend time in silence or in prayer, we start to forget about the things we want or think we need, and we become thankful for the things we already have. Our thoughts and prayers become focused on others as opposed to ourselves, we begin to make conscious efforts to make a difference in the lives of others, and we begin to realize that this is what drives our true happiness.

The feeling that we need to have control in every aspect of our lives begins to fade, and we begin to live with a peace and freedom that our materialistic culture cannot provide.

Our culture is like a salesman knocking on our door trying to sell us something we don't need, and we begin to see that. We can actually get to a point where we feel like we don't need anything or anyone, not in the sense that we don't need our loved ones around us, but in the sense that we don't need anyone to help us experience true happiness. Through our faith we can experience the truest form of happiness realizing that we are responsible for our own happiness, not needing to rely on others to experience that. We will also find that when we do spend that time in silence and prayer, we are often filled with emotions that we don't have the opportunity to express during our busy everyday lives, emotions that will often result in tears of joy and appreciation. We find ourselves laughing and smiling, while at the same time tears are rolling down our face. These are the deepest emotions that we don't come to terms with in any other circumstance.

We need to see these emotions in ourselves to experience a deep, meaningful way of life, and to get to know our true selves better. With that, we can face today's culture with a confidence that we will see things more clearly, and recognize some of the pitfalls that our culture leads us into. We will find ourselves not only avoiding the pitfalls, but praying for others to find it deep within themselves to avoid them as well.

One last difference that growing in a life of faith can make is the way we learn how to handle suffering. We spend most of our life trying to avoid suffering of any kind, and of course, that is a natural human thought. But the fact is that suffering will come our way sometimes, whether we try to avoid it or not. The thing about suffering is that we can be stronger after we get through it. When I was twenty years of age, I was a passenger in a severe auto accident. I was lucky to be alive but suffered some pretty severe injuries. I spent three months in the hospital and did not walk for almost a year. Sixteen surgeries later, I was on the road to recovery. During this time, I spent a lot of time suffering, as would anyone under the circumstances, but there is no doubt in my mind that I am ten times better off today than I would have been had I never gone through that suffering.

When we suffer, it is another opportunity to assess where we are and what we are doing. It doesn't matter whether we suffer physically or emotionally. If we look at ourselves after we make it through the suffering, we are able to see how we are better from the experience. Nobody wants to suffer, but it is inevitable. If we have grown in our faith and we are capable of embracing the times we suffer, we learn from it. We become a better person, and we grow even more in our faith. We also become capable of helping those around us that suffer. We let our experiences, our hearts, and our strengthened faith help make a difference for someone else who is suffering.

Living God's will as opposed to our own is a true way to grow in our faith. It sounds crazy, but sometimes it is God's will for us to suffer. Sometimes that is the only thing that will eventually lead our hearts to Him and to a true life of faith. Trusting the unknown, trusting a life of faith, and making a difference in the lives of others help us to fill the holes in our lives that we used to try and fill with all the material possessions we thought would bring us happiness.

As we grow in our faith, we stop chasing the things that eventually lead us to emptiness. We don't concern ourselves with what the culture tells us, but we become true to ourselves, true to others, and stop chasing the things we thought would make us happy but actually lead to potential pitfalls. It is a freedom that is comparable to no other—to have the strength to avoid the influences the culture presents all of which lead us only to continue to try and fill the holes in our lives. Being rooted in our faith is what leads us to true happiness. To chase true happiness anywhere else is like a hamster running on a hamster wheel. The hamster really isn't getting anywhere, and eventually will get tired and worn down. Wherever we stand in our faith, whether we have none at all or are highly engaged in our faith, it's there whenever we are ready to turn to it.

6

Marriage

FOR BETTER OR FOR WORSE: the vows used in all weddings by the bride and groom during this most special occasion. I have been married coming up on eighteen years, and I consider myself a very lucky man. I am lucky enough to know that my wife and I took those vows literally, and while the majority of the time has been for the better, because we took those vows we are always able to get through the times that are worse.

Our culture has a big issue with facing times that are hard, and it has had a huge effect on marriage and family. We say "for better or for worse," but do we really mean that? When the worst comes, why are there so many divorces? It is almost as if divorce is an option before the marriage even gets started. The mindset that says, *If it doesn't work out, we can just get divorced* seems in place before a lot of us even get started.

WHAT ARE WE CHASING?

At any time in any marriage, there will be times when we are hurt, have a feeling of betrayal, feel unappreciated, and times when quite honestly we do not want to be around our spouse. Remember your spouse has had times when they felt that way about you as well. In a fairy tale marriage, we fall in love, get married, and live happily ever after. Unfortunately it is not very realistic. Sometimes our expectations exceed reality, and we set ourselves up for a letdown when it comes to the way we think our marriage should be. If we realize that we individually change on a daily basis, then we have to understand that our spouse changes as well. We grow and develop based on the experiences we have, and we cannot expect that our spouse won't do the same. In our best-case scenario, we have spent a lot of time searching for the right person whom we believe would be the one we would like to spend the rest of our life with.

In the beginning it is easy to love and accept this person, because he or she is the kind of person you have been looking for. Generally you enjoy the same hobbies, ideas, and like to go the same places. There is really nothing like it when you have found the right person. The obstacles tend to come when one or both spouses begin to change.

As the years start to move on and we buy a house, get jobs, meet new friends, have children, or whatever life brings our way, individually we change. But sometimes in a marriage we don't share the same thoughts on some of those changes. The opportunity to have different opinions or to not agree on certain things increases as we continue to move forward. Many times we don't even know that we have a different opinion about something until a situation comes up that exposes that fact. It is not uncommon to hear experts say that communication is a huge factor in whether or not a marriage will be successful. It may be a cliché to relate communication to successful marriages, but it is a truth that cannot be dismissed. We will always have times in a marriage when we will struggle with communication, but it cannot become the norm if our marriages are to be successful. One thing we have to realize is that we have to communicate even when it may be difficult or we risk hurting the feelings of our spouse. There is often a huge lack of willingness to be completely honest with that person, but then we are left holding on to something that we would really like our spouse to know. A failure to communicate something like that may cause you to have a sense of resentment towards your spouse, because they will continue to not know what it is that is bothering you. Therefore, they have no opportunity to do anything about it. I have heard it said that men feel like they are expected to read a woman's mind. The truth is no matter how well we know someone, we cannot know one hundred percent what another person is thinking, even if that person is your spouse.

Why is it that we struggle so much to communicate at times? It is human nature to want people to see only the things we want them to see and know only the things we want them to know but, for a marriage, that can be a recipe for disaster. We all have things in our past that we regret and generally keep to ourselves, and being in a marriage does not mean we have to lose our individualism, but we should never have to fear what our spouse may or may not learn about us over time.

WHAT ARE WE CHASING?

The true love that is needed to help a marriage continue to evolve must allow for true acceptance of anything we learn about our spouse. When we get married we think we know each other pretty well, and that may be the case with some, but I know that my wife and I know way more about each other today than we did eighteen years ago. In the coming years, we will know even more about each other.

That does not mean that we like everything we learn about each other, but I know that my wife accepts me no matter what, and she knows I do the same. The more we can hand ourselves over to each other, allowing the other to see not only what we want them to see but also allowing them to see our true self with all of our faults and weaknesses, the more we can grow and evolve in our marriage. If we learn something about our spouse that we don't particularly like, it is not up to our spouse to change what we don't like, it's our job to accept whatever it is we don't like. If we choose not to accept it, that's our problem not our spouse's. We cannot control anybody else's choices or decisions, not even our spouse's, but we can decide how we react to those decisions. We can communicate and discuss the choice or decision we didn't agree with, but for better or for worse we must accept it.

Make no mistake about it: there will be times when we will need our spouse to accept us for the poor decisions or choices we have made. As a married couple, it is important to understand that we will all struggle with this, but the reward for excelling in the area of acceptance will result in a marriage that will enhance a relationship to a level we were not aware existed. If we are both working hard to accept one another, then we also get the reward of being accepted unconditionally—and that is when we are capable of thriving the most. When our spouse is not trying to understand our flaws and weaknesses—and is not trying to make us change them but instead is there for us to help us through them—we will begin to have a sense of freedom around our spouse that cannot be matched. We will have the courage to reveal our true self without worrying about the consequences, because there will not be any.

It does not mean that we have a pass to do whatever we want and we should both just have to deal with it, but it does mean that if we choose every day to take our vows seriously, choose to love every day, and choose to accept each other just the way we are—including whatever we learn about each other—we have less of a hesitancy to hold back anything that we hold deep in our hearts. It actually gets to the point where you want your spouse to know all of your flaws and weaknesses because you now have someone to help you with them. So instead of hiding them, you reveal them. It is a sense of relief to be able to share the struggles and weaknesses and to not feel like being perfect is the only thing to strive for.

Two imperfect people get married, and too many times we expect a perfect marriage—that is completely ridiculous! The only expectations you should have in a marriage are what you expect of yourself. We need to be accountable for our own actions and reactions that take place in our marriage. Before we get married we spend so much time focusing on finding the right person for us, but sometimes it would help if we worked on being the right person. Being the right person will help everything else fall into place. If we work on being selfless, accepting, and showing unconditional love the way God shows us, we can't help but find the right person. When we do find that person, it is important that we continue to work on being the right person, until death do you part. The whole line of our most commonly used vows is "for better or worse, until death do you part." We hear these words at many wedding ceremonies and yet so often we struggle when it's worse, and often can't make it until death do us part.

It is surely not the plan as we start our journey in marriage—we mean well going in—but sometimes we just don't know how to be successful, and the culture we live in today is no help. Our culture teaches us to make sure things are going well for ourselves and that something has to be in it for us or else we are wasting our time. Any marriage that abides by this teaching has no chance. If you have a marriage where each person is constantly concerned about "what's in it for me," as opposed to another marriage where each person is concerned about what they could do for the other, which marriage do you think will be successful?

The results of habitually doing things for one another, although not always easy or even sometimes against what you think you should do, are well worth the sacrifice of our own selfish desires. We begin to realize that we get more satisfaction out of doing something for our spouse than for ourselves. We begin to want to do more and more, and that becomes part of who we are. It starts with the little things, and the big things will take care of themselves.

For example, watch a show that your spouse wants to watch. Cook something that your spouse likes to eat. Talk about your spouse's day more than your own. Spend time at places where your spouse wants to spend time. Spend time with family and friends that your spouse wants to spend time with. Bring your spouse a snack while they are watching a show. Take walks with your spouse. Get your spouse a book they would love to read, text your spouse in the middle of the day for no reason. These are just some little things that create an environment for a successful marriage. When the bigger issues arise, being selfless will be less of a challenge. The bigger things will be possible.

Choose to love your spouse every day, and accept your spouse no matter what. Forgive your spouse whenever necessary and as often as necessary. Pray for your spouse every day. The things that are important to your spouse should be important you. We will always have our own opinions, and sometimes we will have a big difference of opinion, but there is nothing wrong with that as long as we accept and respect what is important to our spouse. We didn't get married to our spouse to love and honor them only when they believe the things we believe or do the things we think they should do. We married our spouse to love and honor our spouse no matter what, for better or worse, until death do us part. If you are going to honor your vows and do what you said you were going to do the day you got married, you will love and honor your spouse every day, and even more on the days it may be difficult. It will not be perfect, and there will be times of doubt, times of pain and trouble, but getting through those times is what makes it even better. We often have to go through times of suffering to really understand what we are capable of, and

WHAT ARE WE CHASING?

then when we get through to the other side we understand why we had to go through it.

The problem with what our culture teaches us is that oftentimes before we go through it, we remove ourselves from the situation, never to realize the fruits of what going through some hard times and suffering can bring. Nobody wants to go through hard times in a marriage or in any other part of their life, but the truth is that it does make us stronger, and it helps us grow and develop no matter what stage of life we are in. It is really hard to see the rewards from sticking it out through the tough times while you are in the middle of it, and it takes more courage to go through it than it does to check out. The more strength you can muster up to go through the hard times and the more courage you can find to face the hard times, the more you will persevere, and after each struggle you go through, you will have a little more wisdom for going through it. With that wisdom will come more strength and more courage for whatever storm comes next into your life.

In our marriages, very much like in our lives, there will always be storms, so we need to be rooted in things that will survive the storms: love, acceptance, selflessness, forgiveness, respect, honesty, humility, and most of all, courage. Make these words hold true in your marriage, be courageous enough to go through it all together. In the end, what anyone else thinks, sees, or hears when it comes to your marriage is irrelevant.

In the end, it will always be you and your spouse who will have to live with any decisions made regarding your marriage. It's not easy, and it's not supposed to be. It is hard work, and the messages of today's culture make it harder. We need to be committed to our marriage, we need to work at it, we need to make time for it, we need to be accountable in it, we need to be forgiving, and we need to do all the things that our culture falsely portrays as weakness.

We don't need bigger houses, newer cars, fancy vacations, or any of the material things our culture pushes on us to be happy. We need to be able to sit in a room with our spouse doing nothing. We need to just be there for our spouse, we need to listen more than we speak, we need to spend time with our spouse with no plan or agenda, with no expectations, no distractions. Our spouse needs to come before our jobs, our hobbies, and before our personal wants and desires. We need to have hopes and dreams with our spouse, and we need to strive to achieve those dreams together. There is no magic formula to a successful marriage. Choose to love and accept every day, be committed to self-sacrifice, be there all the time and stay true to your vows, for better or worse, until death do you part.

7

Acceptance

I TALK ABOUT ACCEPTANCE A LOT because I see the difference it makes in people. The funny thing about acceptance is that it is something we desire so much from others, yet it is one of the hardest things to give. There are three areas we need to look at when it comes to acceptance: self-acceptance, the acceptance we receive from others, and the acceptance we offer to others. Self-acceptance is really the key element in all of it. It takes years for us to accept ourselves and, without it, it is impossible to thrive in the other two areas of acceptance. Our culture is the driving force behind the negativity that gets in the way of our own self-acceptance. We live in a time with high divorce rates, broken families, and broken homes. And it is all so publicized now through so many social media outlets that it is almost impossible to be self-anything other than self-absorbed.

WHAT ARE WE CHASING?

We try to teach our kids to be accepting, but a lot of times their parents can't even accept each other—how, then, will our kids learn to accept themselves? We are flooded with ideas saying that bigger is better, the newest is always best, more is the way to go, busier is more important, and if we are not doing something every second of every day, we are going to miss out on something. As much as our human nature leads us to judge others, it is our own self that we sometimes judge the hardest. And, for the most part, this mainly takes place when we are by ourselves. We don't want others to know that we judge and struggle to accept ourselves, so we put on the shield of what we want others to believe—that we have it all together and are just fine with ourselves.

The first thing about accepting ourselves that we have to realize is that we have to accept ourselves wherever we are and for whoever we are at this moment in our own life's journey. We don't have to get ourselves all together and reach perfection before we feel like it is okay to accept ourselves. If we do that, self-acceptance will never happen—last I heard, not too many people are perfect. Understanding that our weaknesses and flaws are a part of who we are is a huge factor in developing our own self-acceptance.

We don't have to understand why we have a certain weakness or flaw, but self-acceptance will be much more successful when we recognize those weaknesses and try to eliminate or improve them the best we can. Getting to know our flaws and weaknesses helps us to get to know ourselves better. It helps us dig into the core of our very being and allows the raw emotional freedom that we so often hold back to come out so that we can be exactly who we are in whatever circumstance we may be in.

Self-acceptance allows us to free ourselves from the cultural onslaught that we so often get caught up in and try to live up to. There are, and always will be, things about ourselves that we don't like—maybe we overreact, maybe we fly off the handle, maybe we get caught up in gossip, or maybe we are hyperjudgmental. Whatever it is about ourselves that we don't like, it is not going to change or go away overnight. But by openly accepting ourselves having these flaws, we give ourselves an opportunity to work on them. Some of our flaws may never go away, but the awareness and acceptance of them will help us to contain the urge to display the behaviors these flaws may produce. One of my biggest flaws is that I am extremely impatient. I am impatient with my kids, which is not all that uncommon, but my reaction to a spilled glass of milk or a hole in the wall today is a much different reaction than it would have been ten years ago—my kids can vouch for that! Ten years ago my kids would have run for cover, but my awareness of the reaction that my impatience has the capability of producing has helped me to change the way I react to a moment of impatience. Maybe I am a little more patient now, but a lot of it has to do with the fact that I have accepted that this is an issue for me, and I am more aware of the situations that cause the impatience.

Of course, there are a lot more serious issues that we could have that would make it challenging to accept ourselves. Maybe we drink a little more than we should, maybe we look at things we know we shouldn't look at, maybe we don't treat

WHAT ARE WE CHASING?

people the way we want to be treated, or maybe we have an addiction of some kind. Whatever it is that we deal with deep in our hearts, whatever it is that we struggle with when we are alone somewhere, deep in our own thoughts, and whoever we are during these times is the person we have to accept. It can actually be a humbling experience to open our own heart and soul, but it is also a burden off our own shoulders to be okay with ourselves just the way we are, with all of our flaws. We no longer have to prove anything to ourselves or anyone else for that matter. Now, that is something worth chasing. We also realize that we can thrive in spite of our struggles, and even more so because of our own self-awareness and acceptance of our own weaknesses. We no longer feel the urge to have to carry ourselves in a certain way or portray a certain image, because we are able to accept ourselves in whatever circumstance we are confronted with. We realize that we do not have to be a certain way, look a certain way, have certain things or have a certain personality and demeanor to accept ourselves.

I believe the success of self-acceptance is what can help us with the second form of acceptance—the acceptance or lack of acceptance we receive from others. One of our biggest urges is to be accepted by others. There is something in our DNA that makes us feel better when we are accepted, so much so that we will do things we may not otherwise do just so we will be accepted. We think we need the acceptance of others for our own happiness. It is kind of silly when you think about it—we spend time doing things and being a certain way so that someone else may be happy with us, but sometimes the things we are doing do not even make us happy with ourselves.

The difference is that when we become successful at self-acceptance, we no longer depend on or have the dire need for the acceptance of others. We realize that not everyone is going to accept us for whatever reason, and we are okay with that.

Accepting ourselves trumps worrying about whether or not others accept us. It is not that we do not want them to, or that our human nature doesn't still wish for that acceptance, but they now have to accept us for who we are and not who they think we should be.

No matter what we do, how we live, or how good our intentions are, someone will always be judging us and not fully accept who we are. Even if we have a strong focus on not being judgmental, it is almost as if our human nature will not allow us to be totally free of that weakness. Even if we do not judge verbally, our mind has a hard time not passing judgement. If we think about the people we love the most, we still have thoughts in our head about how they should be or how they should handle certain things. So, knowing how hard it is for people to not be judgmental, we have to know that there will be many people who will judge us and have a very hard time accepting us. So how do we handle that? We must still accept them for who they are and where they are at that moment. We must work hard not to judge them for not accepting us, we must understand that wherever they are in their journey of life and whatever experiences they have been through have made them who they are today. And if that means they do not accept us for who we are, then we can thrive by accepting them anyway.

WHAT ARE WE CHASING?

The great thing is that we may actually have a huge impact on the person who does not accept us. It will seem odd to them that even though they do not accept us, we still treat them with kindness and great acceptance, and it may have them considering why they struggle with accepting and the underlying issues that prevent them from accepting us just as we are. The reaction we have to someone who does not accept us is up to us, and the impact we can have on someone can be powerful simply because of the way we react.

When I look back on people who had a huge impact on my life, many of them were a part of my life when I may have done things or been involved in things I shouldn't have, and yet they were still there. They accepted me where I was, and some of these people are the people I am most grateful for today.

In our lifetime we must go through the worst of the worst and the best of the best to become all we are capable of becoming, and everybody around us must do the same. We should accept people whether they accept us or not, we should accept ourselves especially when we are struggling to do all the right things. We need to accept that we are human, and that's all there is to it. The weight that we often carry on our shoulders is there because we put it there. We burden ourselves with unrealistic expectations, and we are fueled by the expectations we allow our culture to put on us as well. We often strongly disagree with things people do, what they say, or what they believe, but that it is no reason to not accept them.

I'm sure that many people disagree with some of the things I do or believe, but that's just a part of life. I'm okay with who I am and as for everybody else, I can't control that and I'm okay with that. I definitely do not always understand everybody in my life, and even in my own house for that matter, and when they do something that may really have me scratching my head, I realize that they look at me the same way sometimes.

We cannot control anyone else's actions or reactions no matter how much we would like to, especially in our own circle of family and friends. But we can control our own. We may not be able to control certain emotions, but we can control how we react to them.

A major part of acceptance is understanding that there will be many things that happen that we cannot control. We need to be okay with that. No matter what happens in life and what struggles we are dealing with, the sun will rise and set the next day so as long as we are here, we may as well make the best of it.

Acceptance of others is an idea that took me a long time to process. In my earlier adult years, when money and possessions were still all of the rage to me, accepting others was probably at the bottom of my list. If you did anything to me or around me that caused any kind of negative impact or emotion in my life, it would be likely that I would have nothing to do with you. I found myself putting up walls that people could never break through because I wanted nothing to do with anybody who affected me in that manner. If you disappointed me one time, or caused me any kind of discomfort whatsoever, you would be talking to me through that wall I built to protect myself from ever allowing you to do that to me again.

When we react so harshly to somebody whom we have trouble accepting, we are failing to put ourselves in their shoes

WHAT ARE WE CHASING?

to consider why they may do some of the things that hurt us or that we disagree with.

There are many people in my life today whom I gave plenty of opportunities to have trouble accepting me, but they accepted me anyway. They looked at some of the questionable decisions I made and some of the reactions I had to situations that were less than perfect, and understood that those decisions were made because of whatever experiences I had up to that point in my life. If I were a person who was not accepting, I wouldn't even have been able to accept my younger self at times. That fact alone helps me realize how important it is to accept others.

In contrast to what our culture teaches us, put your own thoughts aside and consider the thoughts of others. We are sometimes so sure of our own opinions that we forget it is exactly that—an opinion. Opinions develop from our life experiences, and our life experiences are all different and always changing. Even our own opinions will change, and sometimes opinions we thought we would never change will change one day. So does everybody else's opinions.

Accept people where they are. Make a list with the names of people you have trouble accepting: family members, friends, coworkers, people you bump into every day, and anybody else you can think of, maybe a bank teller who is slow handling your transaction, or a waiter who is struggling to provide good service, or anybody who could cause you to be unaccepting. Make this list of people and then put yourself in each one of their shoes. Think about how much of their life experience you are actually aware of. In a lot of cases we have very little idea, if any, of where they have been and what they have been through. Maybe we have an idea with some family members and some friends, but even in those cases we have only a little idea of what struggles they sometimes hold in the depths of their heart and soul.

So when you put yourself in the shoes of these people, hopefully you begin to realize the fact that you have little idea why they do the things they do. Yes, sometimes we encounter people who are lazy or appear not to care, like an uninspired waiter at a restaurant or a stone-faced teller at a bank, and our first human reaction is to be annoyed by what we would consider to be bad service. We just have to realize that we have no idea what they are going through and what has made them the way they are. Instead of acting with our first human reaction, maybe we could take a deep breath and just ask that person what their name is and where they are from. Maybe a kind word from us is something that can help make a difference for this person. Whenever you go in most grocery stores, most of the employees have name tags on. What a different demeanor they have when you just say hello and call them by their name. They may get the feeling that they are no longer just some person who works there, but that they are a person with a name who can smile and feel relevant in whatever they are doing.

Everybody we encounter has a story. They are all human souls who have been molded by the life experiences they have encountered. I'll give you an example that had a really powerful effect on me.

About a year ago, I left a business that I had owned for about fourteen years. In the time I was there, there was a store down

WHAT ARE WE CHASING?

the street I would often have to go to for supplies needed for the business. Just about any day I would go there, I would see a homeless man on the edge of the parking lot and he would be collecting money, food, drinks, etc. When I would go in the store, I would often grab a sandwich or water to give him on the way out. Until about five or six years ago, I never said much to him. But, for some reason this one day, before I went in the store, I pulled up next to him and started talking to him. I asked him what happened and how he ended up in this predicament. I wasn't sure what kind of response I would get or if I would get a response at all, but it became one of those moments that changed how I see things. His eagerness to talk and tell his story surprised to me.

His name was Bruce, and he told me many things about his family and some of the circumstances that led him to where he was that day. I would say that Bruce was about forty-five going on sixty, as it was clear that he had been in this predicament for a while. He told me about struggles he had with drugs and alcohol, and how many of his mistakes had caused alienation from his family. His parents lived out on the West Coast and his sister, who lived in the area, had allowed him to live with her, but his inability to get a job due to his history made that too much of a strain. Bruce had a child whom he had not seen for twenty years and had no idea where he was. As he told me all this he shed a tear or two, but it was clear that he knew he brought a lot of this on himself. There was an odd sense of peace that he portrayed in having the feeling that he was less of a burden to everyone by just being in the predicament he was in.

Bruce then proceeded to tell me that he wasn't just out there collecting food, water, or money for himself, but for several other homeless friends who lived with him behind a gas station down the road. I was a little skeptical about this, but also a little curious, so I asked him if we could go over to "where he lived," which was surreal in itself, and I could meet these friends. He was more than willing to show me over there, and I realized he was not making this up. He told me there were about seven or eight people back there behind that gas station so I went in the store and bought enough sandwiches, waters, snacks, etc., for the group. When I came out of the store, I met up with Bruce and he told me exactly where it was before starting to walk down the place, saying he would meet me there. I told Bruce to hop in the car and I would just drive him down there with me. I could see by the look on his face that Bruce was surprised that I would allow him in my car, but he hopped in and we drove to the parking lot beside the back of that gas station. As we got there and I realized this guy was not making this up, I remember thinking how crazy this all seemed to me, and I was anxious to actually meet these people.

As we got out of the car, we began to carry the supplies down the path that led to the area where they lived. Bruce called for a couple of his friends to come help carry the bags of food and water. That's when I met Foot and Debbie, who—after seeing their faces—I realized I had seen at the same store collecting for the group as well.

Their setup was interesting, as they had a large dirt area set up with raggedy tents and blankets, with old chairs and small tables they had clearly found thrown away somewhere. It

WHAT ARE WE CHASING?

was surrounded by so much natural brush and trees that you would never know they were back there. It was clear that they had been there for years, and as I sat in one of those raggedy old chairs and talked to them for about an hour, my whole perspective changed.

That homeless man I used to see all the time was no longer just a homeless man. His name was Bruce, and he had parents who lived across the country, he had a son he hadn't seen, he had a sister in the area who tried to help him, and he had seven or eight friends in the same predicament, all with stories of decisions they made that took them so far off the track.

The strange thing about these people is that they all had this odd sense of peace about them. They were like a small community—they ate together, they were laughing, telling stories, and they were more than willing to let me in on all of it. They would shed a tear if they talked about some of the things that led them to where they were now, but they were not looking for sympathy.

Before I left they were so thankful for the food and water, but they were definitely more thankful for me just sitting there talking with them, accepting them with the human decency that every soul desires more than anything. I accepted their offer to pray with them before I left, and they all shook my hand or hugged me before I headed out—something that probably would have grossed me out an hour before, but not anymore. I loved talking to them. I loved listening to their stories and raw emotions.

Let's face it—nobody wants to be homeless, and it's not like they planned out this path, but the experiences they had and the decisions they made led them to where they were. When we can wrap our head around the fact that every human soul is just as relevant as the other, no matter what their circumstance, then we will really be getting somewhere with acceptance. One person running a multimillion-dollar corporation is no more relevant than one of those homeless men or women sitting in a raggedy old chair. They both have a story, they both have struggles, they both have families, they both have a heart and soul that search for happiness, and they both sometimes go down the wrong path trying to find it.

About once or twice a week I would go see my new friends behind the gas station, bring some food, sit, and talk. I would tell my family about them often, and we actually would all stop by and see them sometimes. After the initial shock, my kids really got a different perspective as well. When we would go, Bruce and his friends would talk to my kids about school and their hobbies just like anybody else. My kids began to ask me if we could stop by and bring them lunch. They actually took hundreds of dollars they had earned from pet sitting and we went and got a list of supplies Bruce and his friends needed as it got closer to winter. We brought blankets, sweatshirts, jeans, waters, hats, and whatever else was on their list.

My one daughter came with her guitar one day to play and sing for them. It helped my kids realize that these people weren't so different. They surely made some bad choices, but we all do. When acceptance is hard, we just have to realize that we don't know people's story. We don't know what leads them to do the things they do. We haven't walked in their shoes. I thought I was being helpful by bringing some food and water

WHAT ARE WE CHASING?

to my new friends, but the reality of it is my acceptance of them is what they enjoyed the most, and also what helped me see things in a totally different light.

I am a better person because of what I learned from my friends behind the gas station. Our culture teaches us to want to be liked and want to hang out with the rich and successful people, to idolize movie stars, reality stars, and millionaire athletes, when, truth be told, we would all do better and learn more from hanging out with people like my friends behind the gas station. They helped me to try harder with acceptance, to try harder not to judge or criticize. They put a clear focus on the fact that life is short, and they are making the best of their situation. They can teach us all a lesson on making the best of our situation when we complain about all the things we want but don't have. Life is what we make of it.

Acceptance of self, others, and not changing so others will accept us makes our life much simpler, and it keeps us from the pressure of having to act or be any certain way. I don't care who you are, what you wear, what you drive, where you live, or what you struggle with. I accept you, and I hope you accept me. But if you don't, I am okay with that too, but I hope you will one day.

8

Humility

I REMEMBER WHEN I WAS TWENTY-ONE how important I thought I was because I was promoted to a manager in my company and found myself making a substantial amount of money at such a young age. I was in a company with multiple locations, and we used to have manager meetings once a month.

The meetings were normally filled with about sixty managers throughout the company, with the majority of them being a good bit older than me. As I look back on it now, you couldn't fit any more ego into that room if you tried. Success does require confidence, which normally comes from knowledge and experience. Confidence breeds enthusiasm, which often breeds success.

WHAT ARE WE CHASING?

There is a fine line, however, with confidence and ego. A confident person is secure in who they are and what they believe, but that person does not believe that they have to prove anything to anybody. They do not feel threatened or defensive when challenged by another person in any matter, and they are not uncomfortable when proven wrong. They do not have to have the last word, and their confidence is often quiet. However, you can be a confident person and cross the line to develop an ego bigger than the room you are sitting in.

The big ego often needs to be fed, and searches for affirmation and constant approval. The big ego is prideful, wants to prove its greatness over and over, and thrives on the admiring thoughts and words of others. I am sure many of you, like myself, have been on both sides of the line. And once the line is crossed, we can get lost in the monster we have created. It's hard work carrying around that big ego, being so self-important and self-promoting.

The big ego often cannot be wrong, and is certain that it has the right point of view. It is defensive and will often not worry about the toes it steps on to continue to feed itself. The confidence someone once had that was attractive to others has developed into an ego that now repels others.

It is a very fine line. The good news is that when we have crossed the line, there is a way back: humility. Not a popular trait in our current culture, it is often mistaken for weakness or lack of confidence, but nothing can be further from the truth. Humility requires more courage and confidence than any other quality. It requires the ability to accept the opinion of others, even though they may be the complete opposite of your own. It requires you to often remain silent, even if you have the answer to a particular situation or problem.

Have you ever had a conversation with someone when you felt like it was a contest to see who could have the last word? Maybe someone is telling you about a great place you should go on vacation, a great restaurant you should try, or what kind of car you should buy. Often, our reaction is to tell that person where we think they should go on vacation, what restaurant we think they should try, or what car we think they should buy. It is like we end up trying to trump each other on who knows better. Why do we do that? I am not sure, but it fits right in with human nature's desire to always seem like we have it together and know what's best.

When people are telling us something, we often fail to realize that even though what they are saying may not seem important to us, it is very important to them. If we did realize that, maybe we wouldn't stick our foot in our mouth so often.

One thing I learned early in my professional career was that I would accomplish a lot more and be more successful by listening rather than talking. Being in a sales profession, the perception is that you would have to be a good talker—have the gift of the gab, so to speak. Nope, not even close. Think about when you are going somewhere to buy something. Do you want someone to tell you everything they know about what they are selling, or do you want someone you can express your needs to, and then try to help fulfill your needs?

We need to be good listeners, and it helps if we realize that people don't want to hear everything we have to say. As a listener, that means we will often be listening to things we

WHAT ARE WE CHASING?

aren't necessarily interested in, but we must remember that it is important to the person we are listening to.

Part of being humble is making things that are important to somebody else important to us. It also means that what is important to us does not need to be pushed onto anybody else.

Being a good listener encourages people to express or reveal things that may be hard for them to talk about. When I realized how much better off I would be by becoming a good listener, it became a huge contributor to the early success I experienced in my professional career. When I was promoted to management, one of my responsibilities was to speak with any customer who my sales team was not able to get a commitment from. I remember one of the members of my sales team telling me that it used to drive him crazy how I would go sit with his customer and there would be moments of awkward silence. I did not go over to the customer and try to talk them into buying something, but I would ask them a question or two regarding their needs and then wait for an answer.

The objections of many sales cannot be solved if we never hear the objections. We closed many sales with people who suggested they were not interested in buying something right now not because we were great salespeople, but because we listened to the objections and the needs of the customer and were able to help them see ways to fulfill their needs. Oftentimes, customers would end up buying something just by talking themselves into it. Just by listening to them and letting them talk through their needs, they were able to come to a decision on their own about what to buy. I have seen many salespeople who were good talkers, and I have watched them talk their way right out of a sale.

These lessons that I learned early in my professional career have helped me to be a better person today. Being a good, humble listener, although not always easy, is often how we get to know people in great depth. We learn what people need and what makes them tick, what they struggle with, and what they are passionate about. It helps us to open up our own hearts, and we can't help but be more compassionate and selfless. We learn that some people are very similar and have the same struggles that we do, and they also have many of the same hopes and dreams. We learn that some people are very different from us, and we gain perspectives that we have never had before.

Now I will admit when I was younger I really didn't want to know all that much about anyone else, and I really didn't see why I should care. I was so self-absorbed that getting to know anyone else on that level was of no interest to me and seemed like a waste of time. That thought process robbed me of so many opportunities to have people be an impact in my life.

We never know what we will learn about others that may impact our own lives. It's not like I go out and try to learn everything about every person I come across, but I am now more understanding when I find myself in a situation where someone is telling me something that is very important to them. When we realize that no matter who we are or what we do is no more important than who anyone else is or what anyone else does, we can learn to embrace humility. It is not easy, and when we do embrace humility we will often be put in situations that will challenge us to remain humble. We will be surrounded by opportunities to speak our mind and to try and prove ourselves, but do we have enough awareness to realize that humility might be the best answer in any given situation?

Developing a habit of humility is difficult and was definitely a lot of work for me. Being put into a management position at a young age gave me the authority to make decisions and no matter what I decided, that decision stuck. That led me to believe that the decisions I made in my profession were always right. It led me to believe that my personal decisions were always right as well, and I always knew best about many things.

Unfortunately, as I look back, that is not the case, and many years of that kind of thinking left very little room for humility. It seems like in today's culture we thrive on getting credit or getting noticed for everything we do and for every decision we make. Sometimes we even do things just to get noticed or get the credit. Our culture teaches us that. It teaches us that the more often we are noticed the better off we are, but that is just not the truth. It often takes us farther away from our true selves.

Growing in humility takes intentional effort. We can start by just doing little things in our own circle of influence with our own friends and family. Do a chore in your own house that somebody else normally does without that person even knowing who did it. Walk past something you want to buy and instead buy something somebody else wants and give it to them with no expectations. Drop dinner off on someone's porch that you know is struggling without leaving your name. These are just some small examples of intentionally trying to grow in humility.

We don't need to be thanked or noticed every time we do something, and we certainly don't need to be right all the time (which is a good thing because we're not). I've learned over the years that although we may have an opinion about something, it's not always wanted or needed and that's okay. If we are successful or good at something, nobody has to know that either. It is actually quite refreshing to find out how good somebody is at something but meanwhile you had no idea. I'll give you an example.

Let's say you have been going to a particular church for ten years or so, and you have a friend whom you have gotten to know fairly well over that period of time. One Sunday while you're at church, this friend gets up with the choir, sings a solo, and has the most beautiful voice you have ever heard. You didn't even know that friend could sing! Something like that just blows us away, and something about the fact that we didn't know anything about it makes it even better.

Our culture teaches us that if you are great at something, everyone should know about it: post it on social media, send messages, text pictures—those are what our culture is feeding off. The practice of humility helps us to not buy into all that. We don't need all that. If we put ourselves out there like that, we have a culture that is just dying to knock us down. In most circumstances humility is not a natural human response, but I think the better we become at it the more peace we have, and the more accepting we are.

As our culture persuades us to run around trying to prove everything to everybody, avoid the temptation to be sucked

WHAT ARE WE CHASING?

in. Step away from the chaos of trying to keep up and always putting your best foot forward.

There is a great calm that rests within a humble soul. It knows how to enjoy the quiet, and it carries with it a peaceful demeanor that encourages us to slow down in this crazy world. It puts in perspective the things we think we need versus the things we really need. It helps us keep our priorities straight, and it helps us recognize the small things that really make us happy. Humility is hard, but the peace it can bring to us makes it worth fighting for. It may be hard to practice humility, but it is just as hard to try and hold ourselves to the standards and expectations our culture has created for us. So we can chase the chaos and standards our culture tries to force upon us, or we can chase humility which will bring us peace and solitude. What are you chasing?

9

The Change

SO IF WE LOOK AT ALL THE TOPICS we have covered up until this point, how do we work on these things to make the changes that will likely go against the persuasion of our society in order to reach a truer self and a truer happiness? How do we look in the mirror and learn to be completely honest with ourselves? How do we become better and more focused on our relationships? How do we become better parents? How do we become less focused on money and possessions and focus on the things that really are important? How do we grow in our faith without the fear of the backlash it may present? How do we become more selfless in our marriages and become better spouses? How do we learn to be more accepting of others? How do we develop habits of humility? This is all important, but do we have the ability to see things with a different view?

WHAT ARE WE CHASING?

There is one thing we all need in order to make the changes necessary in the areas that we know deep in our hearts need to be changed. It's not something anyone else can give us, but we all have it somewhere deep within us: courage!

Making the enormous changes we know that we may need in certain areas of our lives takes courage. It takes courage to look in the mirror and be one hundred percent honest with ourselves. It takes courage to look at ourselves and admit our mistakes—mistakes we make in our relationships as parents, in our marriages, or in our desire for money and possessions. It takes courage to grow in our faith, to make the changes necessary, and to walk away from things or people you have never walked away from before in order to become a better person. It takes courage to be accepting of others no matter what, to be patient, to be kind beyond what our human nature leads us to. It takes courage to be silent when we know we have the right answer, to be humble, and make sacrifices for the benefit of others.

I don't think we can make *any* serious life changes without courage. Some days we may feel courageous, but some days things just get the best of us and leave us feeling tired and worn down. If that's the case, get up the next morning and be courageous again. Sometimes we wake up with it, and sometimes we really have to dig down deep to find it.

Oftentimes we live our lives in fear instead of being courageous. We conform to living in a manner in which our culture teaches us to live out of the fear that we won't fit in. We stay in a comfort zone that fails to challenge us and stunts our growth out of fear of failure or fear of looking bad. We often are just trying to get by, and we miss the opportunities each day to thrive and live up to the true potential that rests inside all of us.

The extraordinary potential that each one of us possesses often goes unknown for an entire lifetime because of fear, and we are busy just trying to fit in. It's really a tragic thought to think about how short our life is here on earth, and how often we let the opportunities to thrive and make a difference pass us by.

Courage doesn't just save lives by jumping in a pool to save someone from drowning, or by pulling someone out of a burning house. When we find the courage to talk to someone we haven't been able to talk to for a long time, or when we are able to listen to someone we haven't really heard before, even though they have been talking to us all along, that may change a life just as much as jumping in that pool or running into that burning house.

People around us struggle, often wearing a mask that says everything is okay, but in the meantime parts of some of the people around us are dying inside, and they need someone to have enough courage to save them. We don't have to be world travelers to make a difference in the world. We could walk across the street to the neighbor or down the block to the homeless man. There are people we cross paths with every day, and parts of them are dying inside. The culture has made them believe they best keep that to themselves, lest they be viewed as weak or needy. All the while, those of us judging that person feel the same way sometimes.

WHAT ARE WE CHASING?

The sad truth is that we never get to know the true potential of some of these people around us. We live with them, we work with them, we walk next to them yet we never get to know what they hold in the depths of their hearts, and they often never know what we hold in ours. Out of fear we hold back our true selves and, in turn, we don't get to know the people around us in that way either.

We need to have the courage to be true to ourselves and accept our own vulnerabilities, being comfortable with people knowing them as well. When we have the courage to show our true selves, it gives the people around us the courage to do the same, and we will be amazed at how much we learn about the people around us and about ourselves. We can begin to live a life focused on the things in our heart that are truly important and not focus on what our culture thinks is important.

This culture doesn't care about us or what we hold deep in the depths of our hearts. It doesn't care if we thrive or if we are fighting for survival. The culture goes on eating us up and spitting us out, and then going on to the next generation. It is impersonal and driven by the love of material things instead of the love of each human heart that struggles each day to make sense of their own lives. Why do we continuously try to keep up with a culture that is spiraling out of control and doesn't have a care for us in the world? What does it take for us to have the courage needed to step back from the pace this culture has created and recognize that we have no reason to chase it or try to keep up with it? If we try to keep up that pace, life will pass us by without any true purpose or understanding. There are many people around us in our families and in our circle of friends who are on this crazy train ride the culture is driving, and sometimes we just have to have the courage to jump off.

We need to have the courage to say: *I am finished with this ride and I am going to tend to things that I have been missing out on, the things that are really important. I want to find out what the best possible me is capable of, without sacrificing what I hold deep in my heart and soul. I want to have discipline and avoid the recklessness we see in our culture today. I want to have the courage to forgive and avoid the vengeance we see in our culture today. I want to live a deep and meaningful life as opposed to the examples of shallow lives we see lived in our culture today. I want to have the courage to be humble instead of what I see in this self-promoting culture. I want to see all people as equally important, regardless of their status or level of success. I want to be a friend with the ability to listen more than speak. I want to be a husband and father who loves unconditionally and always puts my family before myself. I want to help the people around me reach their goals and achieve their dreams, even if it means sacrificing some of my own. I want to have the courage to admit my mistakes, to recognize the times I have failed and hurt others, and I want to learn from those times. I want to have the courage to avoid procrastination, I want to be bold and make a difference in the lives of others.*

We need to find sources of inspiration that help our courage to move us to take action. We don't have much time. We often think we do, but one day we will only have one day left to live, and we don't know when that will be. So if you had one day to live, what would you do?

If you had one day to live, who would you call? Call that person now.

WHAT ARE WE CHASING?

If you had one day to live, what would you want tell your family? Tell them now.

If you had one day to live, where would you go? Go there now. If you had one day to live, who would you want to forgive? Forgive them now.

If you had one day to live, what would be important to you? Make that important now.

We have so many things competing for our time. I promise they can wait. Turn off the noise. When we say no, we are not missing anything. We don't have to keep up with anything or anybody. For me, faith is a huge reason I have learned about the peace of living a life of simplicity. I can look forward to the times when I can sit quietly, pray a little, and read something that will inspire me. This often replaces the times when I used to fill my life with noise and busyness. The truth is I don't miss any of the things I used to do that kept me so busy.

Priorities do change as life moves along, and I think they should. If we don't grow in wisdom over the years, we are missing out. We learn that in reality, we are one hundred percent responsible for our own lives. When we get thrown a curve ball in life, it's up to us how to react. Nobody else is responsible for that. We don't need all the stuff this culture has us chasing. We need courage. Courage to chase the things we hold in the depths of our hearts and souls. What are you chasing?

ACKNOWLEDGMENTS

Thank you to my wife and best friend, Jennifer, and our four children, Maria, Bella, Dominic, and Jack.

Thank you to the 2015–2016 OLOL Youth Group. Being youth minister has inspired me to want to make a difference in the lives of others.

IN MEMORY OF

Father Andrew Vollkommer, dear friend and beloved pastor of Our Lady of the Lake.

www.ingramcontent.com/pod-product-compliance
Lightning Source LLC
Chambersburg PA
CBHW071518040426
42444CB00008B/1704